CLASSIC CITROËNS, Vol. 1
TRACTION AVANT
1934 – 1957

James L. Taylor

1994

Published and distributed by:
YESTERYEAR BOOKS
60 Woodville Road
London NW11 9TN
(081-455 6992)

ISBN 1-873078-16-1

CONTENTS

Printed in England

INTRODUCTION

There was a very simple reason for writing this book: when I tried to find one dealing with the Traction Avant back in 1982, I discovered that there was no complete history available in English. I determined then to write such a book myself, and hoped to have it in print in time for the car's Fiftieth Anniversary celebrations in 1984. Sadly, no British publisher was willing to risk a book on the Traction at that time, and my book remained a series of notes.

In the meantime, some excellent books on the subject appeared in France. There seemed precious little new that could be said about the Traction after Olivier de Serres had published his seminal *Le Grand Livre de la Traction Avant* in 1984, but many people commented to me that there was still a need for a Traction book in English.

So here it is. It is the book I wanted to write in 1982, made infinitely better by being able to draw on the published researches of de Serres and others. What I have tried to do is to tell the story of the car's development and production in as much detail as is compatible with readability, and I have also tried to interpret the reasons behind the changes which were made in production. Where these interpretations are wide of the mark, I accept full responsibility.

I did receive a lot of help in pulling this book together. In particular, I must mention those members of the Traction Owners' Club who offered helpful criticisms, or lent photographs and other reference material. They are (in alphabetical order) Fred Annells, Martin Nicholson, Steve Reed and Bernie Shaw, and they can in no way be blamed for the use I have made of their help. In addition, Citroën Cars in the UK provided some help with pictures, and my publisher Daniel Young came up with some further illustrative material. My thanks go to all of them.

James Taylor

SEPTEMBER 28, 1951   *The Autocar*   27

CITROEN
for *SPEED*
and *SAFETY*

THE ORIGINS OF THE TRACTION AVANT

Before the arrival in May 1934 of the revolutionary Traction Avant (which is simply French for "front-wheel-drive"), Citroën was known as a manufacturer of well-made, reliable and simply-engineered cars. The 1933 "Rosalie" range consisted of four- and six-light saloons of pressed-steel construction, mounted on a conventional chassis available with 8, 10 or 15 CV engines, again of conventional design. They were the logical descendants of a range which had begun when André Citroën had set up as a car manufacturer in Paris at the end of the 1914–1918 War.

Citroën himself was not a Frenchman at all, but the son of a Dutch-Jewish diamond merchant who had set up his business in Paris. Born in 1878, André Citroën earned himself a place at the élitist Ecole Polytechnique twenty years later, and joined the French Army as an engineering officer in 1900. In 1904, he left the Army to set up a gearwheel manufacturing business with two partners in Paris.

Citroën's genius seems to have been in production methods, and in 1908 he was called in by the Mors concern as a consultant to streamline its motor car production. Then, as a Captain in the French Army Reserve, he was called-up on the outbreak of War in 1914. On arrival at the front, he found that his unit – like most others – was suffering from a severe lack of shells. He rapidly sketched up a plan to mass-produce shells, gained official approval of the scheme and, with the assistance of the Armaments Ministry, was able to purchase 30 acres of market gardens on the Quai de Javel in Paris, where he built a vast armaments factory which was turning out 55,000 shells a day by the time the War ended.

When peace came, Citroën thus found himself in possession of a huge factory equipped for mass production with modern American machine tools. He had already made a study of American mass-production methods, and was sure he could turn his knowledge and expertise to advantage. Not surprisingly, Citroën saw his chance to emulate Henry Ford's achievements in the mass-production of motor cars and, equally unsurprisingly, he chose as his immediate objective the emulation of Louis Renault's achievements in France. By the early 1930s, he had not only succeeded in equalling Renault's achievements, but was actually producing more cars than his rival.

It was from this position of strength that Citroën began to think about his future model policy. So far, he had drawn heavily on American examples, but there had been nothing unconventional in any Citroën design. Yet in 1931, two events pushed André Citroën towards the concept of a radically new car, a car which would be quite unlike the conventional cars which he had built until then, and one which he hoped to sell in enormous numbers.

The first of those events was a visit to Renault's Billancourt factory, where Louis Renault had invited him to inspect the massive expansion which was then under way. Citroën was impressed, but he must also have been worried: with facilities like these, Renault would be able to produce far more cars than he could, and would be able to reclaim the number one position in the French market-place.

This visit must have set Citroën thinking. What he would need to maintain his lead over Renault would be a car which was very much in advance of anything his rival could make. If it really was advanced, in design and specification, it could be kept in production for longer than a conventional car before it became outmoded; volumes would thus be higher, and manufacturing costs, in the long run, would be lower. Moreover, a really advanced design would create a very special image of the company which produced it, and this appealed to Citroën, who had always had a flair for promoting his own products.

It was the second of those two 1931 events which provided Citroën with the basis of an idea for the advanced product he needed. Towards the end of the year, he paid a visit to the Budd company in Detroit, whose all-steel method of body construction he had pioneered in France in 1925. At the Budd premises, he was shown an astonishing prototype car which had been built to demonstrate the company's latest method of monocoque body construction.

The monocoque construction itself saved weight, permitted a reduction in overall size without loss of interior space, and was claimed to be cheaper than conventional separate-chassis construction. But perhaps the most intriguing feature of the Budd prototype car was the fact that it had front-wheel-drive, a layout which was still rare in the early 1930s. Budd's chief engineer, Joseph Ledwinka, had chosen to use it because it allowed the car's overall lines to be lower and made available to the occupants that space taken up by the transmission tunnel on a rear-wheel-drive car. Not one of these advantages was lost on Citroën. He returned to France with a licence to manufacture monocoque body shells on the Budd pattern, and with the idea of front-wheel-drive firmly planted in his mind.

Over the next few months, Citroën probably toyed with the idea of introducing a front-wheel-drive monocoque car to replace his existing Rosalie range when those cars came to the end of their production life. The idea seems to have developed, too, and before too long Citroën was thinking of incorporating all the very latest engineering advances into this car in order to give it the commanding technological lead over Renault which he believed he needed. Not only that, but he wanted it in production as soon as was humanly possible.

However, not all of his colleagues shared his enthusiasm for the project. His advisers were pessimistic about the length of time it would take to develop such a car, suggesting that it could not possibly enter production before October 1936. That was far too late for Citroën, who wanted to have it on the market by the spring of 1934 – more than two years earlier. There was also strong opposition to the scheme from Charles Mauheimer, Citroën's financial adviser, who could see only too clearly how expensive the development programme for such a radically new car was likely to be. But André Citroën had the bit between his teeth; he brushed aside all objections and went ahead.

However, Citroën knew that he did not have all the talent he needed within his own engineering department. Chief Engineer at the Quai de Javel in the early 1930s was Maurice Broglie, an ex-Renault man whose own bent was towards the application of conventional engineering solutions. Broglie was clearly not the right man to design and develop the radically new car Citroën had in mind, and so the company chief resolved to draft in another engineer.

It was Gabriel Voisin who found Citroën the gifted and imaginative engineer he wanted. The man's name was André Lefebvre, and he was then working for Renault. He had been with Voisin's own car manufacturing business until Voisin had sold out to Imperia in 1931, and he was now looking for a change from the rather stultifying atmosphere at Renault. If Citroën wanted to build a front-wheel-drive car, then Lefebvre was the ideal man for the job: he had worked with Voisin on a front-wheel-drive project and had also designed a front-wheel-drive car himself, although this latter had never progressed beyond the drawing-board. Citroën liked the sound of what he heard, and so it was that Lefebvre found himself installed in an office at the Quai de Javel with two assistants, and in charge of the new front-wheel-drive Citroën project. The date was 1st March 1933, and on that day the Traction Avant project may be said to have begun in earnest.

The rest of the Traction Avant development team then began to gather around Lefebvre. Like him, they had been hand-picked: Citroën either diverted them from other activities within his company or engaged them specially for the job. The key figures in the team were Lefebvre himself, engine designer Maurice Sainturat, suspension engineer Maurice Jullien, stylist Flaminio Bertoni, and body engineer Raoul Cuinet. It was Lefebvre, however, who laid out the overall design for the new car, which was referred to within the engineering department as the PV. These letters stood for "Petite Voiture", or "small car", a name which was probably inspired mainly by the low-slung construction which Citroën wanted.

The task which Lefebvre's team faced was a tough one. Citroën was adamant that he wanted his new car

on sale in the spring of 1934, which left the design team just over twelve months to get ready for production a car in which everything would be new – bodyshell, engine, gearbox and transmission layout. In fact, they worked incredibly fast. The first prototypes of the PV were running by the end of August 1933, and the car entered production on schedule, just seven and a half months later.

The key feature of the Traction Avant was always its monocoque construction, but it is not clear how directly this depended on the example of the 1931 Budd prototype. The monocoque which Raoul Cuinet designed actually consisted of two major elements, which were welded together. The first of these was a one-piece body shell, and the second was a heavily reinforced floorpan-and-front-bulkhead structure. The front of this was swept forward to form the sides of the engine bay, and from each of these protruded a pair of arms, to which the detachable front subframe assembly was bolted. The idea behind this remarkable piece of design was that the engine and front suspension would be swiftly removable as a unit if required, although in practice it often took as long to perform this operation as to remove the engine in the conventional way.

On the design of the body, Cuinet worked very closely with Flaminio Bertoni, a young Italian sculptor whom Citroën had engaged specifically to ensure that the radically new engineering which went into the car should be matched by exciting and attractive styling. To some extent, it was Cuinet who had to lead, as the PV was Bertoni's first-ever car design, but the distinctive, flowing lines of the body which resulted from their collaboration were a testimony to the impact the Italian had on the project.

Cuinet probably encouraged Bertoni to keep as close as possible to the 1931 Budd prototype's design in the early stages, if only because there was insufficient experience of monocoques at Citroën for him to know what changes he could safely make. In the end, there were still striking similarities between the two cars. Both the shape of the wings and the side profile with its long wheelbase and wheel-at-each-corner layout are very similar, and the overall shape of the Budd car is so unlike that of other early-1930s designs that it is hard to imagine Bertoni could have found his inspiration anywhere else.

In the 1931 Budd monocoque prototype, the long wheelbase and wheel-at-each-corner layout had been designed primarily to increase space within the body. However, André Lefebvre and Maurice Jullien recognised that this layout could also give exemplary ride and roadholding characteristics, and they based their suspension design around it. As the springing medium, they decided to use torsion bars, which had already appeared in the front suspensin of the Rosalie models.

At the rear, Lefebvre and Jullien chose to fit two transverse torsion bars in conjunction with the "dead" axle, while at the front they decided on longitudinal bars. The front suspension was independent – then still rarely found outside America – and consisted of an upper wishbone which pivoted on oil-less bearings, with a swivel pin between the wishbone and a single lower arm connected to the torsion bar. Movement of the lower arm was controlled by friction dampers on the first cars, although this rather archaic system gave way to telescopic shock absorbers after some eleven months of production. As neither rod nor cable-operated brakes could be made to work satisfactorily with an independent front suspension, a Lockheed hydraulic braking system was fitted.

Low though they undoubtedly were, the production Traction Avant models actually sat some 44mm (1.75 inches) higher on their suspension than Lefebvre and Jullien had planned at first. In the original design for the car, the exhaust emerged from the right-hand bonnet side panel, in order not to take up valuable space underneath the body. It was a good idea in theory, but not in practice, because the interior became filled with exhaust fumes as soon as the right-hand side windows were opened. In consequence, the exhaust was re-routed conventionally underneath the body, and the body was raised on its suspension in order to make the necessary room.

Maurice Sainturat, the engine designer, had joined Citroën in 1929 after working for Hotchkiss, Donnet and Delage. Sainturat was one of the greatest French automobile designers of the inter-War years, and the four-cylinder design he proposed for the PV was characteristically forward-looking. Not only was it a wet-liner design, when no wet-liner engine was yet in mass-production, but it also incorporated overhead valves, which at this stage were still a feature exclusive to American cars and to the more expensive European models. It thus brought to Citroën's new volume-production saloon a specification which was unheard-of in the car's intended market. Against this, the traditional (presumably side-valve) alternative put forward by Citroën engineer Jouffroy never stood a chance. There were a few development problems with lubrication and overheating, but the engine was a going concern by the autumn of 1933. At the same time, work started on a V8 engine – effectively two four-cylinders on a common crankcase – which was intended to power the most expensive PV derivatives.

In Lefebvre's original layout for the PV, the engine was installed with the flywheel at the rear, and the drive was taken by bevel gears and a shaft to the gearbox, mounted under the engine. From here, an output shaft led to a worm-drive differential mounted ahead of the engine block. An obvious disadvantage of this layout was its height, and it may have been this which persuaded Lefebvre to scrap it. By the time of the first prototypes, he had turned the engine back to front and repositioned the gearbox ahead of it, with a quill shaft taking the drive back to the front differential. This was the layout which went into production in 1934.

The production gearbox, however, was not the one Citroën had originally wanted. He had set his heart on a bought-in automatic transmission developed by the inventor Robert Dmitri Sensaud de Lavaud and shown in prototype form at the 1932 Paris Motor Show. As a publicity exercise, a C4 and a C6 Citroën had been equipped with this "turbine" transmission for a run across the relatively flat lands of northern France. The stunt had gone without a hitch and Citroën had instructed his engineers to fit the Sensaud de Lavaud transmission to the first five PV prototypes.

Unfortunately, that run across northern France had given a false impression of the transmission's capabilities. Tests with the PV prototypes showed that it worked well on level ground, but that it overheated and ceased to function altogether on hills. It was in March 1934 when the PV development team finally acknowledged that they could not make the automatic transmission work. They arranged a make-or-break test on a hill at Meudon, to the west of Paris, and when all five PV prototypes failed to reach the top of the hill, they informed Citroën that it would not be possible to put the car into production with the Sensaud de Lavaud transmission.

It was fortunate that they had already started work on an alternative manual gearbox, as the PV's launch date was approaching fast. Citroën gave them two weeks to get the PV running with its new gearbox, and they were able to achieve this by fitting elements of the 8CV Rosalie model's gearbox into the casing of the Sensaud de Lavaud transmission. By the time the car went into production, the only evidence of this last-minute change was the hastily-designed gear linkage, which the Citroën engineers laughingly referred to as the "Eiffel Tower". As for the gear lever, that too earned a nickname: the cranked rod which projected through the dashboard was known as the "mustard spoon".

Front-wheel-drive cars demand constant-velocity joints at the outboard ends of their drive shafts, in order to allow drive to be transmitted while the front wheels are turned for steering. The original constant-velocity joints for the PV were designed by Jean-Albert Grégoire, creator of the 1927 front-wheel-drive Tracta, but on test these lost their lubricant and seized solid. The PV team next tried American Rzeppa joints, but these also proved unsatisfactory, emitting loud noises if the car was cornered on full lock. Further development did in fact eliminate this problem (the joints were used successfully on the 1935 Cord 810), but development was not finished in time for the PV's introduction. As a result, the idea of using constant-velocity joints was shelved, and a pair of conventional Hooke joints were mounted back-to-back. They needed frequent lubrication – every 600 miles – and their bulk did inhibit the steering lock and give the Traction Avant an enormous turning circle. Later on in production, improved joints were substituted.

* * * * *

André Citroën presented the PV in prototype form to his dealers on 24th March 1934, hoping no doubt that sight of the new car would inspire confidence in the market and drag his ailing company out of the depths of its financial distress. Charles Mauheimer had been right: the car had proved enormously expensive to develop, and Citroën's insistence on an extensive refit of the Quai de Javel factory during the spring of 1933 (he was probably still thinking of Renault's Billancourt expansion) had not helped the company's finances.

Such was the optimism of the dealers when they saw the new 7CV saloon that Citroën shares gained 10% that very day – but those same dealers cannot have realised that the car was still far from ready for production. Final styling details had in fact been settled just two weeks earlier, and there were still scores of items which needed further development. Citroën had promised the car for the showrooms by May, and in order to honour that promise, he had to persuade his engineers to work flat out to get the car right. On 18th April, he showed the Traction Avant to the Press, and production examples started coming off the assembly lines at the Quai de Javel on the following day.

All these first cars were of course 7CV saloons, with 1,303cc four-cylinder engines and four-light, five/six seater bodies. Yet they were just a trailer for what was to come later, because Citroën intended that there should be a Traction Avant to replace every one of his company's existing models. To that end, the engineers under Lefebvre were already developing additional engines and additional body-styles.

The 7CV was to replace the old 8CV Rosalie models; an 11CV would replace the 10CV Rosalies, and an astonishing V8-engined 22CV was planned to take over from the six-cylinder 15CV Rosalies at the top of the Citroën range. There would be two-door Roadster and Faux-Cabriolet (coupé) bodies for the 7CV, in addition to the four-light saloon; and the 11CV and 22CV models would have enlarged bodies with all three of these configurations. Lastly, there would be a long-wheelbase bodyshell which would be available in both four-light and six-light forms.

These figures, perhaps more than any others, demonstrate just how ambitious were André Citroën's plans for his new car. They show that the Citroën engineers were obliged to develop no fewer than seven more bodyshells after they had finished the original four-light saloon; and that they also had to develop two more new engines after finishing the original 7CV type. Citroën's deadlines were tight, too: he wanted the new shells and the 11CV engine to enter production over the summer of 1934, and the new 22CV engine to be ready for the Paris Motor Show at the beginning of October. It is immediately obvious that the cost of introducing all these new variants at once must have been astronomical, and it is equally clear how hard Lefebvre's design team and the Citroën production engineers must have worked to achieve what they did.

Before the Traction Avant came on-stream, Citroëns were of largely conventional appearance. Nevertheless, this 1933 model – a "Rosalie" in France but a Big Twelve in Britain – could claim advanced features like all-steel bodywork, a freewheel and a synchromesh gearbox. The swan symbol illustrated at top right was for the Chrysler-patent "Floating Power" engine mounting system which Citroën then used.

The Budd prototype which André Citroën saw on his visit to America in 1931 had front-wheel-drive and a V8 engine, and had been built primarily to demonstrate the advantages of monocoque construction. This car was undoubtedly the inspiration behind the Traction Avant.

Left. "Le patron" – André Citroën – the manufacturing genius behind the company which bore his name.

Right. André Lefebvre was the inspired designer whom Citroën hired to lead the Traction Avant design team.

In this view of the Traction Avant monocoque, the characteristic "arms" which formed the engine bay and front suspension support are clearly visible.

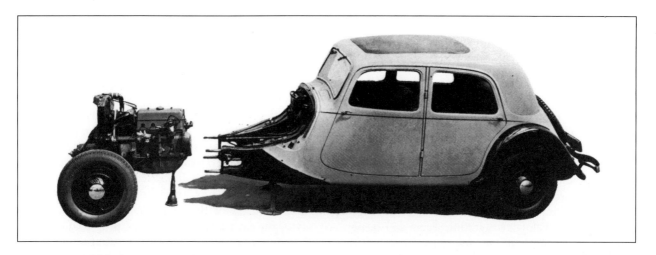

The engine and front suspension unit were designed to be detachable from the bodyshell for servicing, as this picture of a very early car demonstrates.

The original Traction Avant engine was this 1303cc four-cylinder. Later engines had a greater displacement but all followed the same basic layout. Note how the gearbox was fitted to the front of the engine, with the crown wheel and pinion concealed inside the transmission casing and the drive being taken from the rear of the gearbox.

This view of the underside of a 7S model shows the torsion bar springing and the layout of the exhaust, with its tubular silencer mounted transversely ahead of the rear axle.

PANIC STATIONS: THE 1934 7s AND 11s

The last eight months of 1934 must have been a period of frenzied activity in all departments at Citroën's Quai de Javel headquarters. Production of the Traction Avant started in April, and from then until the end of the year, the company was feverishly developing out problems, increasing production levels, and introducing new models. And all the time, the financial crisis which threatened to envelop it was getting deeper and deeper.

The first examples of the new range to go on sale were saloon "7A" types with the 1,303cc 7CV engine, followed by roadsters and faux-cabriolets. Production was short-lived, however, and the 7As were replaced in June 1934 by the 7B with an enlarged 1,529cc engine of 9CV fiscal rating, and by the 7S with an even larger engine of 1,911cc and an 11CV fiscal rating. During September, a proper 11CV model appeared, with enlarged versions of the existing bodies and some new long-wheelbase bodies. Then at the Paris Motor Show in October, Citroën replaced the 7S by the 11 Légère (light 11) model, which was effectively the same car under a more honest designation, and announced the new 22CV V8-engined range. The 7B, 11 and 11 Légère remained in production for the rest of the year, but the 22CV never did enter production and was cancelled at the end of 1934.

* * * * *

With hindsight, it is quite obvious that the Traction Avant had been put on sale before it was really ready, and the first examples of the 7A exhibited some comical failings: bodies cracked, brakes failed, rear axles broke, doors flew open at speed, gear linkages jammed, and wheels were prone to fly off. Yet news of these problems seems not to have reached the public at large or, if it did, the buyers considered the new Citroën had enough merit to warrant taking a risk. Sales were brisk, and figures from the Citroën factory indicate that some 20,000 cars had been sold by the time of the Paris Motor Show in October 1934.

As introduced, the 7A saloon came with a leather-cloth panel in the centre of its roof, a chromed radiator grille with large inverted chevrons behind the grille slats, and the horns mounted on brackets above the front bumper. Unless to special order, wings and wheels were painted black regardless of the main body colour. The rear number plate was mounted above the centre of the bumper, and there was a fuel filler orifice on each side of the boot, which had no external lid and was accessible only from inside the car. The instruments were located in the centre of the dashboard, and the seats – individual at the front and a bench at the rear – were covered in woolcloth.

The 7A roadsters and faux-cabriolets were announced a month or so after the saloons with which they shared their mechanical specification, and entered production in June 1934. While both body styles were exceptionally attractive, neither was of course unexpected in the Citroën range: there had been coupés and open cars in the Rosalie range as well, and most leading French manufacturers of the time offered a range of body styles on each chassis type they produced. In fact, Citroën had originally intended to offer a four-seater open car, but body rigidity proved to be a problem and so development went ahead with a two/three-seater design with a dickey seat. For simplicity's sake, the closed two-door body followed the same lines. Both bodies were styled in Citroën's own studios by Jean Daninos who, some 20 years later, would be responsible for the glamorous Facel Vega cars.

The term roadster was strictly incorrect for a car with proper side windows, but Citroën nevertheless invariably used it to describe the convertible Traction Avant. The cars had a neat-fitting hood which folded away out of sight into a well behind the seats and could be concealed by a fabric cover. They also had wooden door cappings and leatherette upholstery and, unlike the faux-cabriolets, their exterior door handles were fitted below the bright flash which decorated the doors at waist level. Windscreens were arranged to fold forward and to lock in position about two inches above the bonnet, and the rear-view mirror attached to the top of the screen frame was mounted on a pivot, so that it could be swivelled round to remain functional when the screen was folded flat.

The faux-cabriolets shared with the roadsters a dickey seat, which had its release handle behind the front seats and could not be opened from outside. Leatherette upholstery was standard, but real leather was an extra-cost option. The shape of the coupé roof was very similar to that of the roadster's convertible top, and the result was an extraordinarily elegant car. Its appeal seems to have been largely to fashion-conscious ladies, however, with the result that sales were never great.

With any new car design, manufacturers of the 1930s expected teething troubles, and Citroën no doubt expected more than its fair share of problems with the early Traction Avant. However, it does not seem to have expected customers to find the car underpowered. As speed of travel was one of the car's selling points, this was something which had to be put right straight away. Citroën moved quickly and, in June, replaced the 1,303cc 7A model by the 1,529cc 7B and the 1,911cc 7S (or 7 Sport), which offered a power increase of some 35%.

There were no immediately visible differences between the first 7Bs and the 7As, although later 7Bs could be fitted with an all-steel roof at extra cost. All the 7S models, however, had larger tyres and larger headlamps to cope with their higher performance, and two windscreen wipers instead of the one fitted to 7As and 7Bs. Inside, the first examples of the 7S also had ribbed cloth upholstery where the other models had plain cloth. Better trim was available at extra cost on the so-called "Concours d'Élegance" roadster and saloon models, which also had single-colour paint schemes as standard.

Much more significant than these essentially cosmetic differences, however, were the implications of the engine changes. Performance was certainly up – with top speeds of 100kph (62mph) for the 7B and 110kph (68mph) for the 7S contrasting with the 7A's 95kph (59mph). But that was only part of the story. The 1,529cc engine turned the 7B into a 9CV model under the French taxation system, while the 1,911cc engine made the 7S into an 11CV. That meant that both cars were more expensive to put on the road than the 7A had been, and it was probably for this reason that Citroën lowered its prices when the 7B and 7S were announced. That they were called 7s at all was no doubt because Citroën feared renaming the car as a 9 so soon after its launch would confuse the buyers and damage sales. For a time, the trick worked, but it was not long before the public started to call the 1,529cc Traction Avant a "7/9" model.

That Citroën had managed to equip its new car with two new engines in the space of two months was not quite as much of a miracle as it may appear. The 1,911cc 11CV engine had already been drawn up for the forthcoming 11CV model, and the 1,529cc engine was created quickly and simply by using the larger-bore wet-liner cylinder barrels of the 1,911cc version with the existing short-stroke crankshaft of the original 1,303cc engine. An optional ultra-low final drive for the 7B was also introduced to improve its hill-climbing ability, and this was always known as the "mountain" option in Citroën literature. The 7S, meanwhile, had the taller final drive developed for the forthcoming 11CV model.

These two models, each available with the same three bodies as the 7A had been, were enough to hold the fort for the time being. Citroën followed up in August by announcing the new 11CV models to its dealers, and production of these began in September, although relatively few would have found buyers before the model was seen more publicly at the Paris Motor Show in October.

The 11CV, or 11A to give the model its factory designation, did not only offer more power and performance; its primary purpose was to offer more space. To that end, its body had been widened by 12cm (4.7 inches) and its wheelbase had been lengthened by 20cm (7.8 inches). The result was much more room inside, particularly in the rear, and a more imposing appearance which had nevertheless lost some of the delicateness of the 7s. On saloons, the easiest recognition point was the longer rear quarter-panel, behind

which rear seat passengers could lounge in privacy; on roadsters and faux-cabriolets, a longer rear deck helped to distinguish the cars from their 7B and 7S equivalents. It was possible to take advantage of this extra length by ordering a pair of inward-facing occasional seats to fit into the space behind the bench seat which was standardised on two-door 11As. Cars so fitted had no dickey seat unless to special order, although the opening panel in the rear deck remained and served as a boot lid.

Even more space was available in the new long-wheelbase bodyshell introduced with the 11A. This had an extra 18cm (7 inches) between the axle centres, and was available in three configurations. In Limousine form, it had six windows and five seats, with an enormous amount of room between the front and rear rows of seats. In Familiale form, it had the six-window body and either two or three forward-facing occasional seats behind the front bench, which made the seating capacity up to nine; the rear bench was located further back than in the Limousine models, leaving only a small boot space. The third long-wheelbase model was known as the Coupé Limousine, and would always be relatively rare. This had just four windows, a leatherette-covered bench seat with restricted legroom for the chauffeur in the front, and a division. Behind this were two rear-facing occasional seats, and the rear bench was upholstered in velour or cloth, affording its occupants complete privacy behind the large blind rear quarter-panels.

Interior appointments on the 11s were more luxurious than on the 7s. Velvet upholstery was available as an alternative to ordinary cloth, with embossed vertical bands to divide one seat from another, and bench front seats were standard on saloons in place of the two individual seats fitted to 7s. Individual front seats could be had, of course, but at extra cost. There were pockets behind the front seats, side armrests at the rear, and a rear window blind, none of which could be had on the 7s.

Selling the early Tractions

André Citroën had always had a talent for publicity, and in the period between the Traction Avant's launch in the spring of 1934 and the Paris Motor Show that autumn, he set about drawing attention to his new product with typical skill and vigour. On the one hand, he offered hands-on experience to potential customers by sending out on the roads convoys of 7CVs whose drivers were instructed to offer demonstration drives whenever they stopped. And on the other hand, he arranged for the Traction Avant to be the star of a number of record runs, which ensured that the car received the right sort of coverage in the French press.

In July 1934, for example, he arranged for a 7CV faux-cabriolet to be driven around the Montlhéry autodrome for six days non-stop, during which period it averaged 111.203 kph (69mph) and covered more than 16,000 kilometres (9,942 miles). On 17th September, the owner of the Citroën dealership at Fécamp

Classic Citroëns

used an 11CV Familiale to win a local competition for
the maximum distance achieved on 5 litres of petrol.
But the most spectacular publicity was achieved by
François Lecot, a restaurant owner from Rochetaillée-
sur-Saone, near Lyons, who was also an enthusiastic
hunter of motoring reocrds.

Lecot had worked with Citroën before, when he had
driven a Citroën type 35 bus in the Monte Carlo Rally
as a publicity stunt, and he was a natural choice for the
promotion of the new Traction Avant. In the period
leading up to the 1934 Paris Motor show, Citroën
persuaded him to undertake two record runs in a
Traction Avant. The first was a 5,000-kilometre (3,107-
mile) non-stop tour of France and Belgium, which
Lecot managed in 77 hours at the wheel of a 7CV. The
second was an even more spectacular run from Paris to
Moscow and back, this time in an 11CV, which Lecot
undertook during September and October 1934.

The 1934 Paris Show: the 11 Légère and the 22
Citroën had a huge stand at the Paris Motor Show
which opened on 3rd October 1934, and filled it with a
wide selection of Traction Avant models. These
consisted of yet a third version of the 7, the newly-
introduced 11s, and two new ranges, both being seen
for the first time.

The revised 7, which replaced the 7B (although there
was an overlap of models in the showrooms during
October) once again had a new engine. Presumably the
1,529cc engine with its enlarged bores had only proved
a partial solution to the original 7A's performance
problems, for the engine in the new 7C returned to the
72mm bore of the original 1,303cc type and took on the
longer 100mm stroke of the 1,911cc engine. With
1,628cc, the new engine was still classified as a 9CV for
taxation purposes, but Sainturat had managed to
make it rev more freely, and the result was an extra
1bhp some 600rpm further up the rev range as well as
better acceleration from the additional torque provided
by the long stroke. Like the 7A and 7B before it, the 7C
came as a saloon, a roadster, or a faux-cabriolet.

The first of the new ranges was the 11 Légère, which
also consisted of saloon, roadster and faux-cabriolet.
It was a direct replacement for the 7S, and followed
the same formula of the large 1,911cc engine in the
small 7 body shells. However, trim levels were more
akin to those of the larger-bodied 11s. In Citroën
terminology, these cars were 11AL models, but few
people ever called them that. To distinguish the larger
cars from the 11 Légère models, the public coined the
term 11 Normale ("normal 11"), and they would
always be known by that name. As announced, the 11
Légère models had a small "11L" badge on the spare
wheel housing.

If the 11 Légère came as no surprise, however, the
22CV model which Citroën announced as its new top-
of-the-range car must have stunned many Show
visitors by its sheer audacity. Its bodyshells were
essentially those of the 11 Normale cars, but it offered a
claimed maximum speed of 140kph (88mph) at a time

when such speeds were the preserve of expensive
sporting machinery, and it was equipped with a huge
V8 engine – the first from a French manufacturer to
challenge the supremacy of the American Ford V8
which was still seen as an industry standard in terms of
its flexibility and outright performance.

In fact, it appears that the very first 22CV prototypes,
built probably over the summer of 1934, had been
equipped with Ford V8 engines. The installation must
have been problematical, as the Ford engine and
transmission were designed for conventional rear-
wheel-drive cars and would not have been easy to
adapt to the Citroën's front-wheel-drive configuration.
Nevertheless, examples of Citroën's own V8 soon
became available, and prototype testing probably
commenced in September. Meanwhile, Bertoni had
been working on styling changes which would make
the new model distinctive, and a mock-up had been
shown to Citroën's dealers during August.

The V8 engine was once again Maurice Sainturat's
work, and he had designed it so that it had maximum
commonality with the 11CV four-cylinder type. It was,
in essence, two 1,911cc engines on a common crankshaft, although there were many differences of detail.
Citroën literature distributed at the Motor Show
claimed a power output of 100bhp – 15bhp more than
the Ford V8 – and this might not be too inaccurate.
Moreover, according to former Citroën employees, the
3,822cc engine showed up extremely well on test,
offering both extraordinary flexibility and superb
acceleration. One source quotes a 0–100kph (62mph)
standing-start time of 20.6 seconds, which was very
quick indeed for 1934.

The 22CV car itself was more problematical, however.
Early prototypes, probably built with modified 11
Normale bodyshells, showed that the monocoque shell
was not strong enough to cope with the torque of the
V8 engine, and so reinforcements had to be built in.
Similarly, the combined length of the engine and
transmission with its special final-drive unit was
greater than that of the four-cylinder engines, and so
the bodyshell had to be lengthened at the front to suit.
Although the 22CV was the same as an 11 Normale
from the windscreen back, it therefore had a wheelbase
which was 6cm (2.36 inches) longer than its equivalent
on the four-cylinder car, while the actual bonnet was
12cm (5.7 inches) longer. The rear track, too, had to be
widened by 4cm (1.58 inches) to improve stability.

The restyling which was intended to distinguish the
top-model Citroën from its sisters was limited mainly
to the nose of the car. Although this was broadly
similar to that seen on the 7s and 11s, it had a different
grille with a more rounded top and bottom and a
greater number of slats than on the four-cylinder cars.
There was a large "8" in the vee of the chevrons on the
grille, and the long bonnet had single ventilator flaps
on its side panels. Double front bumpers and, most
striking of all, faired-in headlamps with the horn grilles
beneath them completed the front end transformation.
A final touch was a chrome strip on the body sides at

waist level.

There were three examples of the 22 on Citroën's stand at the 1934 Motor Show – a saloon, a Familiale, and a roadster (which was dignified with the rather grander description of cabriolet). A V8 engine was displayed on a stand, and there were examples of the 22 on the demonstrator fleet outside the exhibition hall. As had been the case with every variant of the Traction Avant introduced so far, however, the cars were under-developed. Former Citroën employees have claimed that the extra weight of the big engine caused serious understeer, that handling was suspect, and that the extra power made wheelspin a problem. The extra power and torque would undoubtedly also have put an enormous strain on the constant-velocity joints in the driveshafts. Perhaps one or other of these failings caused the accident in which one of the demonstrators was involved on the third day of the Show. Both the Citroën test driver and the customer with him were killed, and the local mayor forbade the company to make further demonstration runs in his district.

After the Show
The newly expanded range of Traction Avant models attracted customers in droves, exactly as André Citroën had expected they would, but the car's success came too late to save its manufacturer. The cost of introducing so many new models all at once, compounded by the cost of developing-out problems once the Traction Avant had entered production, brought the Citroën company to its knees. Over the summer, André Citroën had tried to raise money from the banks, but without success; he had also tried to pull off an assembly deal for the Traction Avant in Detroit, but his demand for cash in advance had sunk the negotiations. His personal finances, depleted by his passion for gambling, were not enough to shore up his ailing company and, on 21st December 1934, the Société André Citroën was declared bankrupt.

The principal creditor was the Michelin company, which had put a representative into Citroën's head-quarters as early as July to keep an eye on the gradually worsening situation. It was Michelin which now bought the remains of the company, putting in its own top management early in 1935 in the shape of Pierre Boulanger. André Citroën himself was obliged to leave his own company, and he died a broken man in the summer of 1935.

Even as the financial crisis was deepening in the final months of 1934, changes were still being made to the 7Cs, 11 Légères and 11 Normales. The fabric roof panel finally disappeared from the 7C some time around November, and from then on the all-steel roof was standard. At more or less the same time, the horns were repositioned behind the front wings, and small grilles appeared in these to betray the horns' locations. The detail specifications of the 11 Légère and 11 Normale ranges grew closer together and then, in December, a new engine mounting system replaced the "Floating Power" type, and the small swan badge on the left-hand rear wing which had symbolised the Chrysler-patent system disappeared with it. The new "Pausodyne" system, developed for Citroën by Paul d'Aubarède and Paul Lemaire, was essentially a development of the "Floating Power" type, which had in fact been designed by Lemaire in France. Whether it was significantly better than the earlier system is open to doubt, but it did have the merit of freeing Citroën from the obligation to pay royalties to Chrysler.

With the collapse of the Citroën company in December also came the end of the 22CV project. The car had been displayed again at the Brussels Motor Show at the end of November, but development had still not reached the stage where the car could be put into production. After the Michelin takeover, the new management cancelled further development, reasoning that it was going to be expensive to prepare the car for production and that the 22CV was in any case not going to sell in large volumes. Chief Test Engineer Roger Prud'homme has recalled that he was instructed to rebuild the twelve prototypes then at the factory as 11s by changing front wings, grilles, bonnets and engines, and that these cars were then sold off to Citroën factory personnel. Whether this accounted for all the surviving cars has never been satisfactorily explained, however. There have been persistent stories that one or more 22CV prototypes were not destroyed, and the possibility that some would have been on loan to favoured customers supports this; so far, however, none has been found.

This picture of a well-preserved 1934 7C model was taken when it was nearly 50 years old. The black wings and spare wheel cover which came as standard contrast with the lighter (coffee-coloured) body. The rear lights on this car are mounted slightly too low, perhaps as the result of an error made during restoration. Note the folding luggage grid, an aftermarket accessory which was essential on these cars without an opening boot.

The car pictured on the cover of early sales catalogues was probably a hand-built prototype, and differed in a number of respects from production models. Nevertheless, the two forward-opening bonnet vents, the exposed horns and the two-tone paintwork were all standard features of the earliest Tractions.

The early 11CV range consisted of a Roadster, a Faux-Cabriolet, a saloon (the later Normale) and a long-wheelbase model available as a five-set limousine or nine-seat Familiale.

CABRIOLET DÉCAPOTABLE "11"
3 places à l'avant et 2 places dans le spider.

FAUX-CABRIOLET "11"
3 places à l'avant et 2 places dans le spider.

BERLINE 6 PLACES "11"
4 portes - Coffre à bagages intérieur.

CONDUITE INTÉR. 5 PL. "11"
FAMILIALE 9 PLACES "11"

The very earliest faux-cabriolets had the same two-tone colour schemes as the saloons. This is a 1934 11CV model.

This early publicity picture of a long-wheelbase 11CV shows it in rare Limousine form.

The long-wheelbase 11CV Coupé Limousine, or Coupé de Ville, was always rare. This picture is taken from an early sales catalogue, and shows the car's distinctive heavy rear quarters.

The 22CV V8 engine was essentially a pair of 1,911cc 11CV engines on a common crankcase. Note the multiple pulley arrangement for the belt-driven overhead camshafts, the dynamo, and the remotely-mounted cooling fan.

The distinctive front end design of the V8-engined cars is clear on this prototype saloon, pictured at the Quai de Javel factory. Two-tone paint was once again in evidence.

The 1934 Paris Motor Show cars included this red 22CV roadster, which is rumoured still to exist in California.

BECOMING ESTABLISHED: THE 1935-1938 7s AND 11s

Over the next four years, the Traction Avant sold strongly, becoming an accepted part of the French motoring scene. Careful management of the company by Pierre Michelin and Pierre Boulanger put Citroën's finances firmly back in the black, and work began on a new model to replace the aborted 22CV. A number of significant improvements to the existing 7s and 11s were introduced, but costs were carefully controlled and cutbacks in other areas were made to finance these improvements. One effect was that the 7 and 11 Légère ranges became uncomfortably close to one another in both price and specification, with the result that the 11 soon began to outsell the smaller-engined and cheaper car.

It was sad that André Citroën was not around to see the success of his creation, but he would have been both amused and gratified to see that his original publicity claim for the car – that it was two years in advance of anything else on the market – had been amply justified by events. By 1936, in fact, when the Traction Avant had been on sale for two years, that claim was shown to be an understatement, for no other mass producer was anywhere near catching Citroën's technical lead. That the Traction Avant had influenced other manufacturers was nevertheless undeniable – Renault's Celtaquatre and its two-door coupé derivative, Peugeot's 402 range, and the 1938 front-wheel-drive Rosengart "Supertraction" were all evidence of that. Yet the Citroën 7s and 11s remained the only mass-produced cars to feature front-wheel-drive, OHV wet-liner engines, and monocoque bodyshells.

During 1935, however, Citroën was still struggling to get the basic design of the car right, and it was not until the summer of that year that the Traction Avant could be said to be really free of problems. Thus in January, the noisy Rzeppa CV joints used in 7s were replaced by a more satisfactory Glaenzer type, and the 7 bodyshells were reinforced. The 11 Normale soldiered on with its original Tracta-type CV joints until the spring, when it, too, acquired Glaenzer units. In April, all models were given a reworked engine/front suspension unit, and shortly afterwards came cruciform rear axles with a single locating arm in place of the earlier double arms, a new rear cross-member, and telescopic rear dampers in place of the original lever-arm type. The long-wheelbase bodyshells, which had a distressing tendency to bend in the middle, were heavily reinforced underneath at about the same time, and the two-door bodies were given broader decorative flashes on their door tops; the reason for this is unclear, but it must have been a convincing one for the change to be made during this period of austerity at the Quai de Javel!

In the face of all these necessary revisions to cars which were already in production, it must have been extraordinarily difficult for the new Michelin management to make the savings which were necessary to put the company back on an even keel. Revenue from sales of the car itself helped a great deal, of course, but from the summer of 1935 it became obvious that, having got the car fundamentally right at last, the company was now trying to make it cheaper to produce. The new seats which arrived over the summer were the first evidence of this, as they were thinner than the earlier type and built on tubular frames which were also extended above the front seat backs to make grab-rails for the rear passengers. The dashboard was also simplified, and the lighting and horn controls were relocated on the steering column. And, at the Paris Motor Show in October 1935, a painted radiator grille replaced the original chromed type.

Not every change from this period was intended to cut production costs, however, for the Michelin management team was fully aware that it could not rely forever on the Traction Avant's technical advances and that, in the end, the customers had to be offered the features they wanted. So it was that the 7 and 11 saloons displayed at the Paris Motor Show in October had the very welcome addition of an opening boot. This alteration made certain other changes necessary at the rear, and the number plate was relocated to a free-standing plate on the left-hand wing, while the left-hand fuel filler disappeared (leaving the one on the right hand side) and the rear lights were rearranged. In practice, however, the opening-boot body appears not to have become available through the showrooms until the beginning of 1936, and even then a small number of closed-boot shells were built up for sale, presumably to clear old stocks.

Lecot again

The cost-saving drive at the Quai de Javel must have been the main reason why the factory declined to support François Lecot in another of his publicity-gathering record runs during 1935. The original plan for this one had been conceived by André Citroën but, of course, he was no longer around to lend it his support by the time Lecot was ready to go ahead. It was an ambitious project, in which Lecot was to drive an 11CV Traction Avant for eighteen hours every day for a full 365-day year. For Citroën, it would demonstrate the reliability of the Traction Avant; for Lecot, it was another challenge of the type he enjoyed most.

Lecot nevertheless decided to carry on by himself, raising the money he needed by mortgaging his hotel and restaurant business and by attracting sponsorship from various component suppliers. He bought an 11AL, and equipped it with a number of special items. These included a special anti-mist windscreen, a second left-foot accelerator pedal (intended to reduce leg fatigue), two-tone horns and a long-range fuel tank. In addition, he had the car fitted with a radio and with green and red running lights.

On 22nd July 1935, at 3.30am, Lecot set off from Rochetaillée and, accompanied by a representative of the Autombile Club de France who would be present throughout the run to ensure fair play, he headed north to Paris. Once there, he took a brief break, and returned to Rochetaillée, arriving home at 9pm. The next day, he was up early again for a 3.30am start, and this time he headed south to Monte Carlo – the same distance from Rochetaillée as Paris. Over the next 365 days, Lecot repeated this schedule with just two breaks – one in January 1936, when he took a few days off to compete in the Monte Carlo Rally, and the other in June when he undertook a series of visits to the major European capitals, still at the wheel of his 11AL.

Lecot's marathon run ended at Monte Carlo on the evening of 24th July 1936. He had driven exactly 400,000km (248,601 miles), and his car had never faltered. The Traction Avant had been serviced just three times, the engine had been decoked ten times (quite normal for the period), and the tyres had been changed every 25,000 kilometres (15,534 miles). The event made Lecot a hero in France and further boosted the image of the Traction Avant; and today, Lecot's marathon run remains unequalled by any other driver in any other car. That Lecot himself was in his late fifties when he undertook the marathon serves to emphasise the magnitude of his achievement.

The 1936 models
The cost savings continued into 1936. The last of the low-volume Coupé de Ville models was built in December 1935, and from February the saloon models' interiors became considerably more austere; simplified door trim panels for the two-door models followed in the spring. Shortly after that, a single air scoop on the scuttle replaced the two with which the Traction Avant had been launched. Nevertheless, 1936 was the year which also saw the beginning of a steady stream of valuable improvements to the Traction Avant; having got the car right, and having trimmed its specification to keep manufacturing costs within bounds, the Michelin management was now intent on making improvements.

Most notable among these was the arrival in May of a completely new rack and pinion steering system. Such systems were not at all common in the mid-1930s (though one was used on the German Adler front-wheel-drive car), and this one added greater steering precision and control to the Traction Avant's already outstanding handling qualities. It also made the steering rather heavy at low speeds, but the trade-off for greater control at speed was a profitable one, and there was no doubt that the addition of this advanced steering system to the Traction Avant's specification was in keeping with André Citroën's original view of the car as a technological front-runner.

Shortly after the rack-and-pinion steering was introduced on the production lines, Citroën made a number of further improvements to the 7s and 11s. Some were subtle, like the new air filter which lessened intake noise on the 11s, an exhaust modification which affected all models, or the new pedal-box which made the accelerator, foot-brake and clutch lighter to operate. Much more obvious was the redesigned dashboard, for the instrument cluster had been repositioned much more visibly, directly ahead of the driver.

Meanwhile, there had been one strange aberration. Back in September 1934, Citroën had equipped a pair of long-wheelbase 11 models as taxis, fitting them with divisions and with taximeters which protruded through the passenger side of the windscreen. Production did not follow, perhaps as a result of the financial crisis at the end of the year, but in 1936, two further 11A taxis were built from long-wheelbase shells. Whether these were to special order is not clear, but still no production followed. Nevertheless, the long-wheelbase models did become popular as taxis in France during the late 1930s, owners buying either a six-seater Limousine or a nine-seater Familiale and then equipping the cars to suit their own requirements. Of the factory-built taxi, however, nothing more would be heard until 1953.

The year 1936 was also the first one in which the 11s outsold the 7s, and there can be little doubt about the reason. In the specification trimming which had taken place at the beginning of the year, the 11 had been hit particularly hard, with the result that many of the advantages which the 11 Légère offered over the 7 had been removed. That same balance of sales continued into 1937, and for the same reasons. During 1937, the 11 Légère sold five times as well as it had in 1936.

The 1937 models
In fact, January 1937 saw production of the original 11 models, both Légère and Normale, come to an end. Not that their replacements, introduced in February, were very different, however, and the only simple way of telling the difference was by the wheels, which had five studs instead of the six on earlier cars. There were many hidden changes on the new models, though, and these resulted from further attempts to rationalise production and to commonise componentry between 7s and 11s in the interests of minimising manufacturing costs. The revised models were known as 11B and 11BL models, and replaced the 11A and 11AL types respectively. Just one model was not replaced: the long-wheelbase Coupé Limousine, which had sold in only penny numbers and was a costly variant to produce with its unique four-light bodyshell.

During January, 315 of the last 11AL models, with bodies of all three types, were built up as special limited-edition cars. Citroën classified them as 11AM models (the AM possibly stood for AMéliorée, or "improved"). Saloon versions had higher-quality interior fittings, reminiscent of those seen in 11 Légère models built before February 1936, and all types had a revised cylinder head and a Solex 30 DHT carburettor, which between them offered better performance than the standard 11AL had. Quite why this limited-edition was produced is not clear, but it might well have been Citroën's way of clearing old stocks and of testing public reaction to the mechanical alterations: cylinder head and carburettor alterations for both 7s and 11s were in the pipeline for introduction a year later.

Generally, however, 1937 was a quiet year as far as specification changes to the Traction Avant were concerned. Possibly the reason was that the Citroën engineers were heavily preoccupied with the forthcoming TPV car, the "Toute Petite Voiture" ("very small car") which Pierre Boulanger had initiated in 1935 and which eventually materialised thirteen years later as the 2CV. Running changes included stronger drive-shafts yet again for the 7s at the beginning of the year – the sixth different type to be fitted since production of the 7 had begun just two and a half years earlier! New "iridescent" (metallic) paint options joined the range and, at the Paris Motor Show in October, new switchgear demonstrated Citroën's continued commitment to giving the customers what they wanted.

More money was saved, however: from the beginning of the year, all cars came in single-tone paint, and the black wings and wheels of the original cars ceased to be available. In June, the horns were repositioned on the gearbox and the horn grilles were deleted from the front wings, which no doubt made these items cheaper to manufacture. At the end of the year, standard saloon rear doors were fitted to the long-wheelbase cars, replacing their gracefully curved trailing edges (deliberately styled to match the fronts) with the wheelarch cutout needed on the shorter bodies. This standardisation of course saved money, even though the rear side panels of the long-wheelbase body had to be redesigned to suit; no doubt Citroën turned this to advantage, however, and designed in some extra reinforcement.

1938: the Pilote wheel and the Commerciale models
At the 1937 Paris Motor Show, Citroën showed the very first examples of Traction Avants equipped with Michelin Pilote wheels, but these attractive and very practical new items did not become available on production cars until January 1938. The inspiration behind the Pilote was in fact not aesthetic, although there is no denying that the wheels added considerably to the appearance of the 7s and 11s with their large flat radial spokes around a broad centre. It was the Michelin tyre designers who had come up with a new, wide-tread, low-pressure car tyre design in order to improve road-holding and handling, and it was this which was originally designated the Pilote. The new tyre was too wide to fit on to existing wheel rims, and so Michelin designed a special wide wheel for it and, as the tyre company owned Citroën, it was only natural that the new wheel-and-tyre combination should appear on a Citroën product.

The new wheel-and-tyre combination made a very

real difference to the Traction Avant. It lowered the car further, and in doing so of course also brought down the vehicle's centre of gravity. By putting a larger area of tyre in contact with the road, it also offered better adhesion, and the net result of these two factors was a startling improvement in the roadholding, handling and stability of a car which already excelled in these three areas.

The new and wider tyres demanded reprofiled wings, and these arrived in January. The 1937 Show cars and a handful of cars built in early January, however, had the new wheels with the old wings, and the Familiales continued to have old-style wheels until April. As the new tyres altered the rolling radius of the wheels, the 1938 Pilote-equipped cars had lower final drive gearing. Top speed was not affected, but the 1938 models did accelerate rather better than their forebears because the new cylinder-head and 30 DHT carburettor previewed on the limited-edition 11AM models at the beginning of 1937 became standard on all 7s and 11s.

1938 was also notable for the arrival of the new Commerciale model, which used a variant of the long-wheelbase six-light bodyshell. But this was a rather special variant: the whole of the rear end had been reworked to incorporate an opening tailgate which made the car into a versatile load-carrier as well as a capacious passenger car. Although the first prototypes of the Commerciale were built in 1937, series production did not begin until early in 1938. Strictly speaking, the car was known as a Limousine–Commerciale at first, and for 1938 the Familiale was rechristened a Limousine–Familiale, but the names did not catch on and Citroën reverted to their simpler forms for 1939. Limousines for 1938 also came with individual front seats, the bench becoming a special-order option.

The idea behind the Commerciale was of course not new. Dual-purpose vehicles of this kind had been a regular feature of the French motoring scene for many years, for the simple reason that they were ideally suited to the needs of many customers who lived in rural areas. In these predominantly agricultural parts of France, market-towns attracted small manufacturers and merchants of all kinds, and these individuals needed a vehicle which would both carry their wares to market and serve as family transport, for few of them could afford a car as well as a light commercial vehicle. The Commerciale version of the Traction Avant, available of course only in 11CV guise, was designed specifically to meet their needs.

The Commerciale body had been very well thought out. Access to the rear was through a split tailgate, the upper part opening upwards and incorporating the rear window, and the lower part opening downwards and incorporating the spare wheel storage. If long loads were to be carried, this lower part could be fixed in the part-open position by means of chains, or it could be removed altogether. To make loading easier, the rear bumper consisted of quarter-bumpers at each corner, and the rear centre of the car was left clear.

Inside, the attention to customer requirements was

even more impressive. The whole interior – seats, door panels and headlining – was trimmed in black leatherette, and the floor was covered in black rubber. The idea behind this was that the dirt which would be collected when the vehicle was being used as a load-carrier would not show; and if it did, the owner would be able to hose the interior out without damaging it. To that end, a small drain panel was provided in the floor just behind the front passenger seat!

There were two individual front seats, and the passenger's seat could fold forwards against the dash or be removed entirely, or its backrest could be folded flat against the cushion to create a table. Citroën sales literature envisaged this table being used for a pair of scales by an owner who used his Commerciale as a mobile shop. To that end, the interior light was located above the front seats rather than above the rears as in the other long-wheelbase models.

Commerciales came with a bench rear seat which could be repositioned further forwards to create a large boot area and still carry passengers, folded flat to create a large load space, or removed entirely. In the latter case, a false floor could be fitted ahead of the rear axle to give a totally flat rear load area. The rear side doors could be folded flat against the body sides so that an owner could use the rear of his car as his shop window, and the door trim panels were made detachable to prevent damage when bulky loads were being carried. In order to give the Commerciales reasonable performance when fully laden with the six sheep or 200kg (441 lbs) of other goods which Citroën sales literature envisaged, they were given the lower final drive of the standard-wheelbase cars. Otherwise, they were mechanically standard.

There were few other changes in 1938. Paint options were reduced in number, and black became more or less standard on all models except the two-doors, although the iridescent colours remained available as well. A gear lock was added in March, and the faux-cabriolets were marketed from the beginning of the year under the Coupé name. However, they did not last. Only some 700 of all types had been built since production had begun in June 1934, and the model ceased to be available in the autumn, production of the 7C version ending in September and that of the 11s ending in October. Even the Paris Motor Show in October brought no surprises for 7 and 11 customers, and it was not until November that Citroën introduced something new in the shape of a heater. This was little more than a crude air duct which carried warm air from behind the radiator to the passenger compartment, but it was a shrewd move by Citroën to introduce it just before the onset of winter!

The October 1938 Show was nevertheless an important one, for it was here where Citroën announced its new 15-Six model. This was the top-of-the-range car which at long last took over from the 15CV Rosalie which had gone out of production in 1934 and, in the Citroën scheme of things, it replaced the aborted 22CV car. However, as was usual with Citroën at this stage, its announcement at the Show did not coincide with the start of full production: that had to wait until the following February.

Pierre Boulanger took the reins at Citroën in 1935 and oversaw the development of the Traction into the car its creator had always wanted. Ironically, he was killed in a Traction Avant development car during 1950.

The "7C", 1935. (Citroën 30.170-7)

This 1935-model 7C saloon was among the earliest examples to dispense with the two-tone colour scheme.

For 1935, the exposed horns disappeared and horn grilles were fitted into the front wings. They are just visible on this Familiale.

Organes de commande

1. Levier des vitesses.
2. Levier de frein à main.
3. Contact d'allumage.
4. Commande du démarreur.
5. Indicateur de niveau d'essence.
6. Ampèremètre.
7. Indicateur de pression d'huile.
8. Interrupteur d'eclairage.
9. Commande d'éclairage "Phares et Code".
10. Commande des avertisseurs.
11. Commande d'ouverture du pare-brise.
12. Commande des volets d'auvent.

The 1935 dashboard, as illustrated in Citroën literature of the time. The glove-box is shown open.

François Lecot and the Traction Avant with which he did his epic 365-day run between Paris and Monte Carlo during 1935–36. The car was fitted with a special anti-mist windscreen.

A Roadster dating from 1935–36, seen here with its windscreen folded flat. The wing-mounted horn grilles characteristic of this period are clearly visible on this single-tone car.

Two-tone cars were becoming increasingly rare by 1937, but this 11BL has the contrasting black wings more commonly associated with earlier models. The forward bonnet side vents were now hinged at the back, and the chromed handles had moved to their leading edges.

1938 cars were fitted with Michelin's new Pilote wheels, designed to suit the company's latest tyres. This close-up, designed to demonstrate the method of jacking a Traction's rear wheel, shows the wheel and its large hubcap.

The elegant Pilote wheels fitted to this 1938 Roadster helped to make the car look longer and lower.

There are Pilote wheels once again on this 1938 Familiale, which has the saloon-type rear doors introduced at the end of 1937 instead of the gracefully curved doors of the earlier long-wheelbase cars.

REALIGNING THE RANGE: 7s, 11s AND 15s, 1939-1945

In January 1939, the Citroën car range consisted of the 7C and 11BL, both available as saloons or roadsters, and the 11B, available as a saloon, roadster, or long-wheelbase Limousine, Familiale or Commerciale. Yet this range was to be short-lived, for the new 15-Six entered full production during February, the 7C gave way to the 7 Eco at the end of the month, and the 11B and 11BL models were superseded by 11B Perfo and 11BL Perfo types during March. In the process, the cheapest roadster disappeared from the range, for the 7 Eco came as a saloon only; the 15-Six was also available only as a saloon at first, but long-wheelbase Limousine and Familiale models followed during March.

This revised range, now weighted more heavily towards the more expensive end of the market, survived the outbreak of War in September 1939, but production began to slow down towards the end of the year. Although 7 Eco, 11 Légère and 11 Normale assembly continued at a low level throughout 1940, the 15-Six was taken out of production that February. Fewer than 3,000 cars were built under the German occupation in 1941, and Traction Avant assembly effectively ceased that year. Four more cars were assembled during 1942, but thereafter no more Traction Avant models were made until the 1945 Liberation.

For 1939, bright colours had all but disappeared from four-door models, and most cars were delivered in sober black; only the two-door models, perhaps more frivolous by nature, could still be had in a full range of colours. As one black Traction Avant looked very much like another, Citroën therefore decided to distinguish each model from the next by the colour of their wheels. While 7s therefore continued to have wheels finished in the body colour, 11 Normales all had red wheels and 11 Légères all had yellow wheels. When contrasted with black bodywork, these two colours actually gave the cars a particularly striking and attractive appearance. Apart from an alteration in the shape of the gear lever surround, which for 1939 lost its rounded corners, these red and yellow wheels were the only specification change before 15-Six production began in February.

The 15-Six

It is not clear exactly when development of the 15-Six model had begun, but the most likely period is the summer of 1936. By this stage, Citroën's finances were once again in reasonable shape, and the Michelin management had begun to look at improving the existing models. It would therefore have been quite in keeping with the policies of the period to begin work on a new top-of-the-range model.

The essence of the 15-Six was of course its new six-cylinder engine, which Maurice Sainturat drew up on the basis of his existing four-cylinder design. Using the same bore and stroke dimensions as the 1,911cc engine, the six-cylinder came out at 2,867cc and gave 76bhp – just 30bhp more than the 11CV four-cylinder. This gave a very much better performance than even the 11 Légère with its big engine in a light body, and the 15-Six was capable of more than 80mph with quite respectable acceleration. Its French fiscal rating was actually 16CV, but Citroën decided to market the car as a 15CV, not least because the last six-cylinder Citroën (which had ceased production in 1934 and was still around in fairly large numbers) had been a 15CV.

With six cylinders, the new engine was of course half as long again as the four-cylinder, and when it was mated to the gearbox used in the 7s and 11s, the engine/transmission unit was far too long to suit the standard bodyshell and front subframe. The earliest prototypes, running in 1937, therefore had lengthened front ends with the radiator grille well ahead of the front wheels, and former Citroën employees have said that they handled badly as a result.

As there was little chance of making the engine shorter, the Citroën engineers set to work on the gearbox, and Forceau and Camusat came up with a new three-rail design which was shorter than the existing type. However, its compact design demanded that the engine should turn anti-clockwise instead of in the orthodox clockwise direction. Sainturat accordingly arranged for the six-cylinder engine to do exactly that, with the result that the new engine became known as a 15G type, with the G standing for Gauche (left), the direction of the crankshaft's rotation.

Citroën had hoped to introduce the 15-Six at the beginning of 1938, but these and other development problems meant that the car was not ready in time. A pilot production run of about 50 cars was made that summer, and these had aluminium wings and bonnets, presumably in order to save weight. However, the aluminium seems to have been considered too expensive, and it had disappeared from the specification by the time the car was announced at the Paris Motor Show in October 1938.

When André Citroën had planned the V8-engined 22CV model as the top of the Traction Avant range, he had made sure that it was instantly distinguishable from lesser models by its unique front-end design. By contrast, the 15-Six betrayed the more sober thinking of Pierre Boulanger, who had taken over as Citroën's President after Pierre Michelin had been killed in a traffic accident at the end of 1937. There *were* front-end differences between the 15-Six and the four-cylinder cars, but they were subtle ones. Most obvious were the bumper overriders, the exposed horns (a reversion to 1934 practice no doubt made necessary by space restrictions), the chromed "15-6" motif which covered the starting-handle hole in the grille, and the louvres which replaced the ventilator flaps of four-cylinder cars in the bonnet sides. The fact that the bonnet itself was also 11cm (4.3 inches) longer than on the 7s and 11s was probably the least noticeable of all the differences.

The bodyshell was essentially the same as that of the 11 Normale, and in fact the prototypes had been developed using strengthened 11 Normale bodyshells. Again there were differences, but again they were subtle. There was a bright trim strip running along the door tops, all but the first few cars had stone-guards on the trailing edge of the front wings and the leading edge of the rear wings, there were semaphore trafficator arms in slots at the top of the door hinge pillars, and there was a chrome "15-6cyl" badge on the right-hand rear wing. Ivory-painted Pilote wheels also served as an identification feature, and contrasted neatly with the black paint in which most 15-Six models were delivered.

Lastly, there was the interior. Citroën's main aim had been to make the 15-Six more luxurious than the four-cylinder cars, and to that end there was dark brown velour upholstery and the rear bench seat came with a central armrest. The dashboard was distinguished only by a pair of vertical trim bars, but the handbrake had swapped sides and was now outboard of the driver rather than in the centre of the car.

The 7 Eco and 11 Perfo models

As the 15-Six came on-stream in February 1939, the 7s and 11s were given improved sound-proofing. However, the old 7C lasted only until the end of the month, when the roadster was taken out of production and the saloon was revised to became a 7 Eco. During March, the same series of revisions turned the 11B and 11BL into 11B Perfo and 11BL Perfo models.

The purpose of these revisions was to realign the Traction Avant range. As the production figures in Appendix C demonstrate, sales of the 7C had started to decline in 1937 and had nose-dived in 1938; the reason was primarily that the prices of the 7C and 11 Légère were too similar, with the result that the majority of customers opted for the more powerful car, in spite of its greater running costs. Noting this preference in the market, the Citroën management decided to separate the two ranges more clearly by making the 7C into an economy model and giving the 11 extra performance. The new names reflected these intentions: 7 Eco was short for 7 Economique ("Economy 7"), while 11 Perfo was short for 11 Performances ("Performance 11"). Of course, it would not have been sensible to leave the 11 Normale short of performance, and so that was modified in the same way as the 11 Légère.

In fact, the 7 Eco was not really a new model, but rather a revised 7C, and the fact that its commission numbers continued the sequence initiated by the original 7C without a break shows that even Citroën

recognised the main difference lay in the way the car was marketed. The physical differences between the 1939 7 Eco and the earlier 1938 7C all lay in the power train: the engine was differently tuned, with a higher compression ratio and a new carburettor, and a special high final drive was fitted. The overall results were that performance was affected very little, while fuel economy improved by 10%.

Like the 7 Eco, the 11 Perfo models were simply revised versions of existing models, in this case of the 11B and 11BL cars. Once again, the revisions were confined to the power train, and in this case to the engine alone. The 11 Perfo engine was nearly 22% more powerful than the 1938 11CV motor, as a result of its improved cylinder head with a raised compression ratio, and its new carburettor with a more efficient tubular air filter. Lighter con-rods and shorter valve stems also allowed the engine to rev more freely, with the result that acceleration was improved, while top speed went up by around 10%. Fuel economy, meanwhile, remained as good as before.

Traction Avant production under the Occupation

The effects of Citroën's range realignment for 1939 were only just becoming apparent when the mobilisation of the French Army to counter the threat from Germany in September threw the automotive industry into chaos. As far as it is possible to tell, however, the strategy had worked: customers had turned away from the 11 Légère and focused instead on the 7 Eco and 11 Normale. Sales of both ranges were up, and the healthy increase in 7 sales had reversed the downward trend which had begun in 1937. The 11 Légère had continued to sell strongly, and no doubt its position within the Citroën range would have become clearer as time went on. As for the 15-Six, its enthusiastic reception had not yet been matched by large sales volumes. Partly, no doubt, this was because the buying public needed time to readjust to the idea of a Citroën option at the 15CV end of the market once again; but the main reason must have been the outbreak of War, which persuaded the wealthy middle-classes who would have been the six-cylinder car's natural customers to put away their money and await better times.

For 1940, with production at low levels to match sales, the same overall pattern was repeated. The best seller was the 11 Légère; next came the 11 Normale and 7 Eco in that order; and the smallest volumes were achieved by the 15-Six. It is difficult to draw any conclusions from these figures, however, for 1940 became even more chaotic than 1939 had been when Germany invaded France during May. Within a month, Paris had fallen and the French Government had surrendered, and in the uneasy peace which followed the Armistice of June 1940, prices started to rise alarmingly.

The 1940 Traction Avant range had been cut back considerably to meet these changed conditions, and instead of sporting major revisions, the 1940 models simply had a token change to the chevrons on the radiator grille, which were now fitted outside instead of behind the slats. It is probable that a 15-Six roadster would have been announced at the 1939 Paris Motor Show in October, as several prototypes were made over the preceding summer, but the War prevented the Show from going ahead. The 15-Six roadster was thus lost forever, along with the original 2CV, of which a pilot production batch of 250 was under construction when War broke out.

In fact, there were no roadsters at all built during 1940; only one 11 Normale Limousine was made in January, and production of the 15-Six stopped altogether in February after just 25 examples had been completed. Times were too hard for luxuries like these. Dozens, possibly hundreds of partially-completed cars were destroyed during the German bombardment of Paris which preceded the French surrender of June 1940, and it was no doubt for this reason that the 7 Eco saloons ceased to be available in June. Nevertheless, 11 Légère and 11 Normale saloons remained available throughout the year, and the Familiale and Commerciale 11 Normales could also be bought. Few customers dared after June, however, not least because anyone seen to be prosperous enough to afford a new car at this time was likely to be accused of collaborating with the German Occupation Forces and to suffer the consequences.

Inevitably, the extraordinary circumstances resulted in the production of some peculiar vehicles. Between March and December 1940, for example, stocks of interiors for the 15-Six models were used up in a batch of 180 11 Normale saloons, which were dignified with the designation of "spéciale peluche" (super plush). As supplies of essential items became difficult during 1941, Citroën offered new cars with four tyres only, and a fifth at extra cost. According to factory records, production of 7 saloons stopped in June 1941, that of 11 Normales followed in July, and that of the 11 Légère – always the most popular model – ceased in November. Prices were established for 1942 cars, and the fact that Citroën was prepared to offer cars for sale *with no tyres at all* shows how desperate the supply situation had become. In practice, however, production had ceased.

Just four cars were built that year, one 11 Familiale in February and three 11 Légère saloons in June. For the rest of the War, the Citroën factories produced only commercial vehicles.

During the German Occupation of France, the Traction Avant acquired a kind of mythical status. The car proved ideal wartime transport for both sides in the conflict: there were thousands of examples in France; spares and servicing expertise were easy to come by; the cars were rugged and reliable; and most versions were also spacious. Immediately after the invasion of September 1939, the French Army began to requisition civilian-owned Tractions for these very reasons, and no doubt recognised its error in failing to adopt the car earlier (it had been unable to do so for bureaucratic reasons – French military regulations stated that Army staff cars had to have a chassis!). The invading Germans, meanwhile, had also started to requisition cars, and before long many examples had been painted or camouflaged in a variety of military styles.

The Germans took over those cars which had been requisitioned by the French military authorities when the French Government surrendered in June 1940, but the Traction Avant remained in demand, this time by the F.F.I. (Free French Forces) and the Resistance. Throughout the German Occupation of France, the Traction Avant remained at the forefront of the fighting, and for many patriotic French men and women, it actually came to symbolise the spirit of a free France.

If petrol and tyres were precious commodities during this period, cars were even more so, and in such circumstances it would not have been surprising to find cars being assembled from stocks of spare parts, or from parts cannibalised from other vehicles. It is quite possible, too, that some complete cars left the Citroën factory without being logged out and without bearing any identifying body or commission numbers. No doubt the licensing authorities in some areas would have turned a blind eye to such abuses, while in others they might have been obliged to provide the Occupying Forces with documents for such cars. The full truth will never be known for certain.

A 1939 Commerciale demonstrates its carrying capacity. The tailgate was in two parts, and there were quarter-bumpers at the rear to allow the lower tailgate to fold downwards.

The 7C was still on offer for 1939, although it had become a 7 Eco by the end of the season. By this time, the 1628cc engine put out 36bhp.

This 1939 model was finished in sombre black, like so many of its contemporaries, but from the side, contrasting red Pilote wheels would have distinguished it as an 11B Normale.

The yellow Pilote wheels mark this car out as an Onze Légère, but the hubcaps would not have been painted in body colour when the car was new.

The 1939 dashboard, as shown in Citroën literature of the time.

The six-cylinder engine was much longer than the four-cylinder type, and so the transmission had to be made shorter in order to fit the powertrain under the Traction's bonnet. This early six-cylinder engine is marked "Essai" ("test"), and was probably used in development.

The 15 was readily recognisable by the louvred sides of its longer bonnet, which placed the radiator grille nearer the bumper than on four-cylinder models. This is the saloon version.

The 15 was also available in long-wheelbase Familiale form. The length of the engine and gearbox unit meant that there was no longer room to fit the horns on the gearbox, so they were once again fitted to the bumper. Overriders were another distinguishing feature of the 15s.

As this picture taken from Citroën literature shows, the six-cylinder models' dashboard was distinguished by a pair of bright vertical strips in the centre.

ANY COLOUR, SO LONG AS IT'S BLACK: 11s AND 15s, 1945–1952

Paris was liberated by Allied forces on 23rd August 1944, and France began the long struggle back to normality. Private car production was not among the highest priorities, and there were in any case severe problems for Citroën, whose factory had suffered heavily in the 1940 bombardment of Paris. Much had been destroyed, the production lines for the Traction Avant had been dismantled, and the company had to start again from basics.

As a result, the first cars did not leave the Quai de Javel factory until June 1945, and these had been assembled mainly from parts in store. As raw materials remained scarce, all of the 1,525 cars built during 1945 depended to a very great extent on old-stock parts. All of them were 11 Légère saloons, and all of them had what was essentially the 1939–1940 specification, modified as necessary in the light of the difficult supply situation. No doubt all kinds of anomalies were created when supplies of the "correct" components dried up and the assembly line workers did what they could with the parts they did have to hand.

The difficult circumstances in which these cars were assembled in any case led to certain specification differences from the pre-War versions. They lacked the rear window surround pressing (which never would reappear on post-War models), their headlamp bodies were painted instead of chromed, and their door trim panels were made of compressed cardboard. And, because tyres were still in short supply, they were sold initially without tyres or with four tyres only at extra cost.

In a France impoverished by War, few individuals could afford a new car, and Citroën rapidly recognised that it would have to look to export sales in order to survive until demand at home recovered. It must have been for this reason that the next Traction Avant model to re-enter production was the 15-Six, which had the power, the luxury features and the roadholding to compete against the products of other manufacturers in the open markets outside France. Citroën announced the return of the six-cylinder car in February 1946, but production would not begin in earnest for another two months.

Within a few weeks of the date when 15-Six production began, Citroën made a number of alterations to the specification of the 11 Légère, with the aim of keeping production costs as low as possible in what was, and was likely to remain for some time, a very difficult economic climate. In some cases, items were commonised between models to simplify production, and thus the 11 Légère gained the overriders and waist-level door trim strips already fitted to the 15-Six. In other cases, the cost-paring was more obvious. Although

15-Sixes retained their elegant Pilote wheels for the moment, 11 Légère models were given Michelin BM disc wheels (the BM name stood for Bon Marché, or "cheap"). Louvred bonnet sides were also specified for the 11s, shorter than those on the 15-Six but no doubt cheaper to produce than the type with separate ventilator flaps.

Still in the interests of simplifying production, Citroën painted the majority of its 1946 models black, although some brighter colours were offered to improve the 15-Six's appeal in the major export markets of Australia, New Zealand, Africa and Scandinavia. To a degree, it seems to have been a case of applying whatever paint was available, but the standard black was supplemented by a pair of "iridescent" greys and a green. Wheels were body-colour on 11s, but ivory on 15s unless the main body colour was light grey, when red wheels were fitted. Upholstery was almost uniformly grey, although velour was used on 15-Six models instead of the cloth on 11s, and dark brown velour was also found on the six-cylinder cars.

Trying to give the 11 Légère additional appeal, Citroën reduced its fuel consumption slightly by retuning the carburettor as part of the May 1946 revisions. Whether this materially helped sales is impossible to say, but the 11 Légère did sell strongly during 1946, and it was probably this which persuaded the company that the time might be right to re-introduce the 11 Normale. A single car was therefore built, and was displayed at the 1946 Paris Motor Show in October as an expression of intent. By contrast, sales of the 15-Six suggested that the company had been over-optimistic about its potential, as only just over 200 cars found buyers during 1946.

After the War, a small number (probably four) of the 15-Six roadster bodyshells which had been built in 1939 still existed at the Citroën factory, and at least two of these were built up as complete cars in 1946. However, both were special-order vehicles for senior Michelin figures, and their construction did not signal any intention on Citroën's part to introduce a production 15-Six roadster. One of the two was built for Robert Puisieux, the director of the Michelin factory at Clermont-Ferrand, and was among the first dozen examples of the 15-Six to come off the lines after the War. The other – a red car – was built for the Michelin family. The Puisieux car was written off in an accident during 1947, but the other still survives in the USA. The fate of the remaining 15-Six roadster bodyshells in unknown, but regular "sightings" of six-cylinder roadsters are still reported and some experts believe that about a dozen 11 Normale roadster bodyshells were converted and built up as 15-Six roadsters.

1947–1949: the road to recovery
During 1947, with the French economy still in a parlous state, Citroën proceeded cautiously at home. Exports became increasingly important and more than 60% of all Traction Avant models built that year went abroad, mainly to customers in Australia and New Zealand, in Africa and in the Scandinavian countries. Larger cars were still difficult to sell, and sales of the 15-Six proved slow in all markets. Some six-cylinder sales were probably lost to the 11 Normale, which became available in March, but which did not sell in large quantities. Fortunately, sales of the 11 Légère almost doubled, with the result that 1947 ultimately proved quite a good year for Citroën.

Just one running change was made at the beginning of the year, when the 11 Légère and 15-Six models then in production had their rear-view mirrors moved from the top of the windscreen to the bottom. From the beginning, the 1947-model 11 Normales therefore had the low-mounted mirror, but they were otherwise essentially the same as the last of their pre-War equivalents. Austerity still ruled, however: the 11 Normales had painted headlamp shells and bonnet handles, and they had no aluminium edging to their radiator grilles. Nevertheless, they did have waist-level trim-strips on their doors and stone-guards on the edges of their wings, both features already being standard on the cheaper 11 Légère models.

There was little scope in these hard times for changes of real significance, however. Most of the company's development effort was going into the forthcoming 2CV model, and only a little was available for modifications to the Traction Avant. In the seller's market of the immediate post-War years, Citroën chose not to tinker with their well-proven design, although they did undertake an important redesign of the six-cylinder model's drivetrain.

From the time of its announcement at the 1938 Paris Motor Show, the 15-Six had used a unique gearbox, and this had made it necessary for its crankshaft to rotate anti-clockwise rather than in the usual clockwise direction. Citroën engineers had now given further thought to the design of that gearbox, and had come up with a new two-rail type which allowed the crankshaft to rotate clockwise. This replaced the earlier type on the production lines in June 1947, and the new car with its clockwise-rotating crankshaft was redesignated a 15-Six D (the D standing for "Droite" or Right and referring to the direction of rotation). These revised models could be distinguished from the earlier 15-Six G by the new starting-handle arrangements in their grilles: the cutout for the starting-handle was now a vertical oblong, protected by a "15-6 cyl" badge above a pair of stylised wings.

Perhaps no more than 30 of the new 15-Six D models had been made before Citroën found it necessary to make revisions to the engine. The poor quality of post-War petrol demanded a lower compression ratio, and with this were introduced a modified cylinder head and a new carburettor. The low-compression models,

known as 15-Six DB types, were introduced at the Paris Motor Show in October 1947.

The Paris Motor Show also introduced a number of smaller changes to the public. A chromed radiator grille surround returned to the six-cylinder cars (although the vertical bars remained painted), sidelights disappeared from their wing tops, and these most expensive Citroëns had a new and simplifed interior finished in grey-blue cloth. Sadly, Pilote wheels were no longer available, and the 15-Six was fitted with the BM disc type with the same small hubcaps already seen on the 11s. Dashboard clocks, missing since production had restarted in 1945, were reintroduced on all models. The Show was also the first opportunity many people would have had to see that 11 Légère models now came with the wing stone-guards already fitted to the 11 Normales and 15-Sixes, although the change had actually taken place in August or September.

The revised Traction Avant range presented at the 1947 Paris Motor Show undoubtedly had been improved, but it is unlikely that these improvements were a significant factor in the very healthy sales figures recorded during 1948. The economic situation was easing, and larger cars were becoming more readily saleable, with the result that there was a greatly increased demand for the 11 Normale and 15-Six models. Greater sales of these models accounted for almost the whole of the 50% improvement which 1948 Traction Avant sales saw over those in 1947. The 1948 sales total was an encouraging one, even though it was way below the pre-War best and still depended heavily on success in overseas markets which might prove volatile.

There had been some sacrifices, however. Four-cylinder cars were now uniquely available in black, and most six-cylinders were also delivered in black, although metallic grey was available as an option. Wheel colours no longer distinguished one model from another, and all 1948 Tractions had ivory wheels. One reason for these changes was undoubtedly to simplify production and thus to save costs; another may well have been that a greater variety of paint finishes was simply not available from Citroën's suppliers.

Changes to the range during 1948 were few and far between, because a large part of the year was taken up with the launch of the 2CV, which was announced at the Paris Motor Show in October. Citroën no doubt considered that the 1947 revisions had been enough to keep interest alive for the immediate future. Nevertheless, the beginning of the year had seen the four-cylinder cars fitted with a new grille which had the same starting-handle cutout as that on the 15-Six, and with grey cloth upholstery as standard. Then, in summer, the 15-Six took on an all-chrome grille and was further modified to become a 15-Six DV. Other changes to this model were not readily visible, however, and affected only the pedal-box, front axle mountings, and crankshaft. Lastly, as 1948 turned into 1949, the six-cylinder cars began to appear with revised wing stone-guards, which had a cross-hatched design.

The year 1949 could perhaps be called the year of the 15-Six, for in a France which was now gradually becoming able to afford large cars once again, this 11-year-old design suddenly took on a new importance. Not the smallest factor in this was that it was adopted as the official car of the French Government – a role for which its elegance and discreet luxury made it admirably suited. Sober black 15-Six Citroëns soon became a familiar sight outside Government buildings and, over the next few years, became almost symbolic of the Fourth Republic administration.

The car also captured the popular imagination. In spite of its age, it was still competitive with the latest large-car designs from the other French manufacturers. What it lacked in straight-line acceleration, it made up for in its cornering and general road-holding abilities, which enabled it to put up some very quick cross-country times on the poor French roads of the day. Its comfort (improved at the beginning of 1949 by luxurious new "Pullman" seats in place of the earlier tubular-framed type) and its general roadability (performance was helped by a raised compression ratio which took advantage of the better-quality petrol now becoming available) earned it the popular nickname of "Queen of the Road". Capitalising on the model's new-found success, Citroën added two features at the October 1949 Paris Motor Show which distinguished it subtly from its cheaper four-cylinder stablemates: side-lights returned to the tops of the front wings and larger hubcaps were fitted.

Sales of the 15-Six during 1949 more than doubled their 1948 levels. Sales of the 11 Normale also improved dramatically, nearly doubling their 1948 levels and closely approaching two-thirds of the levels attained by the 11 Légère, which remained the most popular of the Traction Avant models. These improved sales added up to an overall sales increase of some 40% for the Traction Avant range. Exports remained healthy, although Citroën had been obliged to resort to at least one curious practice in order to satisfy its overseas customers. In many markets, the sober black which was almost universal on the Quai de Javel production lines did not appeal and so, as supplies of brighter colours were not readily forthcoming, Citroën shipped just over 900 Tractions in primer to its overseas dealers. The dealers then had the task of painting these to suit their customers, which resulted in some weird and wonderful colour-schemes!

1950–1952: signs of age
At the turn of the decade, the Traction Avant was riding high in the French market, and export sales were higher than ever before. For a 16-year-old design, this was astonishing. Worldwide sales in 1950 improved on 1949's, 1951's improved on 1950's, and in 1952 the annual total exceeded the best pre-War figure for the first time.

Overall sales figures did not tell the whole story, however. While sales of the 11 Légère and 11 Normale models increased steadily at the beginning of the 1950s,

sales of the six-cylinder car peaked in 1951 and dropped off sharply in 1952. Despite subsequent specification changes, there would be no recovery for the 15-Six; its heyday was over.

Age was at last beginning to count against the Traction. As motoring magazines of the time reveal, its equipment levels were beginning to look distinctly spartan, its comfort levels were beginning to be questioned, and its straight-line performance could not match that of newer designs. The 1950 arrival of the modern-looking but stodgy 12CV Renault Frégate barely harmed the four-cylinder 11CV Citroëns in sales terms, but it did throw into relief the 1930s styling of the Traction Avant. This undoubtedly had a knock-on effect on the 15-Six models. And overseas, where the 15-Six was increasingly coming into contact with much more sophisticated machinery, sales must have been hit hard. Both at home and abroad, those who were in the market for a car as expensive as a 15-Six also wanted one which looked modern, and the Citroën no longer did.

Back at the Quai de Javel, work had already started on the eventual successor to the Traction Avant, and by the early 1950s the new car was beginning to take shape. Prototypes were running, and it did not take long for information to leak out to the press. As so often happens, however, the information was partial or (because of later design changes) misleading, and it may well be that rumours circulating in 1951 of a face-lift for the Traction Avant were the result of this kind of confusion. It was of course true that a redesigned boot was in the pipeline for 1952 introduction, but the suggestion that the front wings were to be redesigned to incorporate faired-in headlamps was probably nothing more than a combination of wishful thinking and partial knowledge of the work then under way on the forthcoming DS.

Real improvements to the Traction at the beginning of the 1950s were few in number. Citroën further distinguished the 15-Six from the four-cylinder models in the summer of 1950 by adding small vent panels on either side of the radiator grille and large bumpers with a straight, ribbed blade which were quite different from those on the 11s. There were interior changes for all models, with new upholstery materials (in a pinkish grey cloth for the 15-Six), decorative horizontal trim bars on the dash, and two-spoke steering wheels. These latter came in on 11 Légère and 15-Six models in the summer of 1950, but the 11 Normale models retained the older three-spoke type until spring 1951. The better-quality petrol now available allowed Citroën to raise the compression ratio on all four-cylinder engines in February 1950, and a new carburettor in May further exploited that advantage, improving both economy and performance. At the same time, a new Vokes air cleaner was fitted, mainly to minimise noise levels; some cars, however, had a Miofiltre alternative.

Further changes were limited partly by supplies difficulties. Home-market cars were still almost invariably finished in black, because there was a shortage of other paints. Overseas customers, perhaps less tolerant of such difficulties than were the French who faced them every day, continued to demand their Tractions in a wider range of colours, and so the numbers of cars shipped abroad in primer for dealers to paint themselves increased considerably. In 1949, the figure had been around 900; in 1950, it more than doubled to over 2,000; and in 1951 it more than doubled again, to some 5,000 cars. Only in 1952 did the figure fall once again, no doubt largely because export sales were beginning to decline.

Supplies difficulties during 1950 were a reminder that things were not yet back to normal in France, and also caused some production anomalies. A strike at the Michelin factories between March and May deprived Citroën of wheels and tyres, and the company therefore turned to its Belgian subsidiary (which assembled Tractions using a percentage of locally-sourced parts) for supplies. Both 11s and 15s built in this period left the Quai de Javel fitted with the Lambert et Nivelles wheels used on Belgian cars, with their 14 oval perforations around the circumference. During the summer, further supplies difficulties were probably the reason why some 11s had a Miofiltre air cleaner instead of the Vokes type, and why some had Zenith instead of Solex carburettors.

Acutely conscious of the Traction's increasing age, and spurred into action by delays in the development of the DS replacement (which had originally been scheduled for 1953 introduction), Citroën planned a whole series of changes for 1952, with the result that 1951 saw no significant modifications at all: only a new oil-pressure gauge on four-cylinder models in January and the introduction of the two-spoke steering wheel on 11 Normales a few months later differentiated 1951 cars from 1950 models.

When the major changes arrived in the spring of 1952, it was quite clear that their main purpose was to enhance the cars' appearance and therefore their showroom appeal. Only the braking revisions on all models in April and the new pedal-box fitted to 11s that month did not fit into this category. Over a period of four months between April and July, the changes were introduced progressively, and it looks as if old-stock parts were being used up at the same time as the new-stock items were coming on-stream. The result was that some Tractions built in the spring and early summer of 1952 had interesting "hybrid" specifications.

New wheels with four slots in their circumferences arrived for all models towards the end of this period, and they retained the ivory paint standard on all models since mid-1947. The wipers moved from the top to the bottom of the windscreen in accordance with contemporary practice elsewhere, and the window frames were modified. Inside the cars, headlinings were changed, plastic lower door trims arrived and some plastic was used in the upholstery of 11CVs. The dash on all models lost some of its ornamentation and was then replaced by a new design with a central ashtray. In addition, the exposed metal parts of 15-Six interiors were painted light grey while the rear seat head cushions were modified. As far as the home-market cars were concerned, all those built after 1st May 1952 were obliged by law to have flashing indicator lamps, and these were fitted to the front wing tops in streamlined housings which replaced the small side-lights. At the rear, the flashers were mounted on the D-pillars, just above the waistline. The most important change of all, however – the addition of the so-called "big boot" – arrived right at the end of this period.

All kinds of curious specifications appeared as production got under way again after the 1939–45 War. This picture represents the 1946 11 Légère as Citroën would have liked them all to be! Louvred bonnets and overriders were now standard on all models of the Traction.

The 11 Normale of 1946, again in a rather idealised form as envisaged by the factory.

The 15-Six D, with its revised engine and gearbox, arrived in 1947. This rear view shows its distinguishing badges.

A 15-Six of 1950, wearing large aftermarket stoneguards on its rear wings. The grille was once again chromed for 1950, and the hubcaps were larger, but the bumpers were still curved.

The 1950-model 15-Six was made more luxurious with the addition of what Citroën called "Pullman" seats. The semaphore turn indicators were not normally fitted ahead of the front doors as they are here, so this car may have been a prototype, or just possibly a Swiss-market model.

For 1951, the 15 was given straight bumpers with ribbed faces. This is in fact a 1952 model, one of the last made before the enlarged boot arrived.

A very interesting French-built 11 Normale, dating from 1951/52. The car belonged to the French Naval Attaché in London, and was converted to right-hand-drive for him to use in Britain. The flashing turn indicators above the front bumper are a discreet modern addition.

The 1951 dashboard, introduced in June 1950, brought with it a two-spoke steering wheel, a cream-faced instrument panel and horizontal decorative bars. The windscreen wiper motor was still above the screen, but the rear view mirror was now mounted on the dashboard.

In this side view, a 15-Six demonstrates the imposing presence which helped it to become the regular transport of French officialdom during this period.

15-Six D engine, 1947.

BIG BOOTS AND HYDROPNEUMATICS: 11s AND 15s, 1952-1957

The "big boot" models started coming off the production lines in July, and were thus available well before the Paris Motor Show that October. It is a measure of Citroën's determination to bolster sales of the Traction that the enlarged boot was not held over until the Motor Show. In fact, 1952 proved to be a record sales year once again, but the company recognised that the writing was on the wall: the Traction would not remain a best-seller for ever and there was no telling at this stage how soon the planned DS replacement might be ready for introduction.

Frankly, the enlarged luggage boot did nothing for the looks of the Traction, but its introduction was an astute piece of marketing. One criticism levelled at the 11s and 15s in recent years had been their uncompromisingly pre-War "two-box" styling, at a time when all new cars were imitating the post-War American "three-box" styling with its separate boot at the rear. Secondly, the boot on the Traction was undeniably small. By introducing the enlarged boot, Citroën succeeded in giving the Traction something of the appearance of the latest "three-box" designs, and at the same time greatly increased its luggage capacity. For an increase in overall length of just three inches (7.62cm), this was a master-stroke, and must have contributed materially to the record 1952 sales figures.

On the four-cylinder Tractions, the arrival of the big boot had been accompanied by new bumpers, which were straight like those on the 15-Six but flat instead of ribbed. For the rest of 1952, however, there were no further changes to the cars; and the picture was much the same in 1953 and 1954. Nevertheless, light green upholstery became an alternative to light grey for 1953-model six-cylinder cars and, towards the end of that year, a few paint options began to appear in the catalogues. Wheels, too, could be had in colours other than ivory. Perhaps in anticipation of these changes, Citroën had shipped fewer cars in primer to its overseas dealers during 1953 (a total of no more than 400, as compared to more than 1,800 in 1952); in 1954, no doubt as a consequence of the new introductions, only some 250 cars were sent overseas in primer. Chromed boot-lid hinges, filler caps and wiper arms introduced early in 1954 were no doubt an extension of the brightening-up process which the new paint colours had initiated.

Nevertheless, 1953 and 1954 did see an expansion of the existing Traction range. The long-wheelbase models, absent from the Quai de Javel production lines since 1943, were re-introduced – to meet customer demand, if Citroën's own word is to be believed. The first to make a comeback was the 11 Familiale, which re-appeared in July 1954; it was followed by the 15 Familiale in September (which, for some reason, had

the old three-spoke steering wheel); and the line-up was completed in April 1954 with the 11 Commerciale, now with a redesigned single-piece tailgate. Unfortunately, production figures for the Familiales are not available, but there cannot have been very many six-cylinder versions. The 11 Commerciale, on the other hand, certainly did justify its re-introduction: over the next four years, its sales were more than double those for the similar period of its availability at the end of the 1930s.

Also made available early in 1954 were Familiales and 11 saloons which had been equipped at the factory as taxis. They came complete with a taximeter, a division, and two-tone paintwork when required. Although the Familiale proved popular as a taxi in France, it is not clear what proportion of those which did become taxis had been equipped as such by the factory when new.

The 15-Six H

The long-wheelbase models were no more than revivals of earlier Traction variants, but 1954 did see the introduction of one model which really was new. This was the 15-Six H, a version of the 15-Six which was introduced in April that year and remained available alongside the "standard" 15-Six for the next two years, outselling it and also outlasting it in production by a small margin. Nevertheless, it did not make a major difference to the overall annual totals of six-cylinder models, which remained at a low level.

Introduced with the 15-Six H were a slightly more powerful engine and an upgraded interior which had Dunlopillo seat cushions, but these were incidental to the car's main purpose. The "H" in its name stood for Hydropneumatic, and referred to its revolutionary new rear suspension. This had in fact been developed for the forthcoming DS models – where it would be fitted to all four wheels – but Citroën had wisely decided to gain some experience of the hardware in service before committing its new car to production with the all-hydropneumatic system.

The new suspension's main advantage was that it offered an extraordinarily high standard of ride comfort without any sacrifice of roadholding. Its only real disadvantage was that it sounded more complicated than it really was, and in fact Citroën's own dealers showed considerable mistrust of it at first. Yet the system proved robust and leak-free in service, thanks to the close-tolerance engineering which had made it possible in the first place.

On the 15-Six H, the whole rear suspension was completely different from that of the standard car. Instead of a beam axle, there was a swinging arm for each wheel (similar in principle to the 2CV's suspension), which could move only in the vertical plane. And instead of the familiar torsion bars, the 15-Six H had as its suspension medium a sphere above each wheel, containing a cylinder with a piston attached to a lever, which in turn was attached to the hub carrier.

The spheres contained hydraulic fluid under pressure, and were connected by tubes to a pressure accumulator which was kept topped up by an engine-driven pump. This in turn drew hydraulic fluid from an underbonnet reservoir. Diaphragms in the spheres separated the hydraulic fluid from a gas sealed into the spheres, and the action of the one against the other provided suspension damping. The suspension's height (or ground clearance) could be altered by changing the pressure of the fluid in the spheres, and this could be regulated by a system of valves, operated automatically by a height corrector or manually by a lever below the dashboard. An additional advantage was that the system could be used to aid in wheel-changing. First, the rear of the car was raised hydraulically; then a support was placed beneath it; then, as the suspension was lowered again, the car remained on the support and the wheel lifted off the ground.

This new rear suspension gave a much softer ride than the torsion-bar type of the standard 15-Six, and to avoid the pitch which would otherwise have been caused by ill-matched front and rear spring rates, Citoгën had fitted the 15-Six H with longer torsion bars giving softer springing at the front. To minimise the cornering roll which came with soft suspension, anti-roll bars were fitted at both ends of the car, with the result that the 15-Six H could corner as quickly and safely as a standard steel-sprung model. Interesting, too, was the substitution of narrower 165 x 400 tyres for the 185 x 400 type on the standard 15-Six: presumably the new suspension made the fatter tyres unnecessary.

The benefits of this remarkable new suspension system were probably most noticeable in those countries where roads were not generally in good repair – in France itself, for example, or on Belgian *pavé*. In countries where the roads were reasonably well-surfaced, its benefits were rather less apparent. Nevertheless, there was no doubt that the system worked, and worked well. So well did it work, in fact, that the basic principles seen in the hydropneumatic rear suspension of the 1954 15-Six H are still being applied in modern Citroëns, nearly 40 years later.

1955–1957: the end of production
After 1952, the French press published so many speculative stories about the forthcoming Traction replacement that the public was well-primed to expect the DS at the 1955 Paris Motor Show. During 1954, expectations were running so high that Traction Avant sales took a serious tumble: many buyers preferred to wait another year for their new Citroën rather than to invest in one which was soon to become outmoded. Despite the fillip which the 15-Six H's introduction provided, therefore, 1954 saw overall sales totals fall to

below their 1950 levels.

The 15-Six H had been in production for just eighteen months when the new DS19 was introduced in October 1955. Primarily in order to cater for conservative customers, but also as a safeguard against problems with the early DS models in service, Citroën kept the Traction Avant range in production for nearly two more years. Such was the success of the DS, however, that Traction sales dwindled rapidly, and by the end of 1956 they had dropped to around half their 1954 levels.

As the new DS was rated as a fiscal 11CV, it was theoretically a direct replacement for the two 11CV Traction models. Sales of both were hit hard, although the decline of the 11 Normale was slower than that of the 11 Légère which had formerly been the most popular model. However, the DS was considerably more expensive than the 11CVs it replaced, and for this reason it also came into the reckoning of those who would formerly have bought a six-cylinder Traction Avant. Few buyers thought it worth paying the extra for the outmoded older car, despite the prestige of its extra two cylinders and, by the end of 1956, the 15-Six and 15-Six H were as good as dead. Overall Traction Avant production was down to around a seventh of its 1953 peak during the first months of 1957, and the assembly lines at the Quai de Javel were finally closed in July.

There were few changes to the 11s and 15s in these last years, and there was little need for any. New lighting regulations in France came into force at the beginning of 1955, with the result that twin rear lamps were fitted to all models and the "15-6 cyl" badge on the right-hand-rear wing of the six-cylinder cars had to be resited on the boot-lid. In May 1955, a new version of the 1911cc four-cylinder engine (known as the "11D" type) went into all versions of the 11, but this did not reflect any desire on Citroën's part to improve the cars. The engine was in fact that which had been developed for the DS after the flat-six originally planned had been scrapped in 1952, and it went into the 11 Légères and 11 Normales purely as a way of streamlining production and of getting some experience of the type in service before the DS went into production.

The 11D engine brought improvements in both speed and flexibility to the 11CV Tractions. Although it was essentially the same engine which Maurice Sainturat had drawn up more than 20 years earlier, it had been extensively redeveloped by its creator. Most important, perhaps, were the redesigned cylinder head and valve-gear. These allowed the engine to breathe more deeply, and were backed up by a raised compression ratio, a modified camshaft, new pistons and rings, and a reinforced crankshaft and shell-type big-end bearings (instead of white metalled bearings) to cope with the extra strains imposed by the increased power output. A new rocker cover had also been designed to make the engine look different from those it superseded.

Traction assembly had already begun to wind down by the end of 1955. The 15 Familiale was the first model to be formally withdrawn, in August 1955, but the standard 15-Six had also become an endangered species by this stage, and the majority of six-cylinder models were ordered with the hydropneumatic suspension option. Citroën remained flexible enough to deal with special orders, however, and during the 1956 model-year provided a unique pair of 15 Familiales with hydropneumatic rear suspension for conversion into Presidential parade cars (see Chapter 7). Cars continued to be delivered to overseas dealers in primer, as even the expanded range of catalogued colours was insufficient for some markets, and in fact the last such cars were built in the final months of production.

The official end of Traction Avant production came on 25th July 1957. The last car off the lines was an 11 Normale model, which had begun its progress down the assembly lines on 18th July and had been appropriately decorated by the production workers on the way: thus, by the time it reached the end of the line, it had a bouquet above the windscreen, a French flag in corrugated cardboard on one door, and a red lamp hanging on its rear. The final touch was supplied by the Citroën publicity department, who painted the word "Fin" (End) on its number-plate, and arranged for it to be collected by Monsieur Dufour, the Saint-Malo Citroën dealer who had sold the very first Familiale in 1934. This car, however, was not the very last Traction Avant to be built. That honour went to one of a pair of

15-Six H models which were handbuilt to special order in November and December 1957. They were despatched without ceremony, and their whereabouts are unknown.

Epilogue
Looking back today, it is all to easy to misrepresent the significance of the Traction Avant. It was not the first car in the world to incorporate front-wheel-drive, a monocoque bodyshell, an overhead-valve wet-liner engine, and torsion bar suspension: all these features had been seen before in limited-production or unsuccessful vehicles. Much more important was the fact that the Traction was the first *mass-produced* car to incorporate all these features, which had come to André Citroën's notice piecemeal over the years preceding its introduction.

The Traction brought to ordinary motorists in France and in dozens of other countries a mechanical sophistication which was simply not available to them elsewhere, and in so doing it increased their expectations of the motor car. Other manufacturers had no choice but to try to catch Citroën's technological lead. That they took so long to do so is part of the fascination of the Traction; but that they were obliged to do so and thus changed the face of motoring in the mid-20th century is the real significance of André Citroën's masterpiece.

Summer 1952 brought several changes. This 11 Normale shows the new straight bumpers, scuttle-mounted windscreen wipers, and flashing direction indicators on the front wings. The wheels also changed at this time, from plain discs to discs with four slots in their outer circumferences; the slots are just visible in this picture.

Most obvious of those summer 1952 changes was the enlarged boot, seen here on an 11 Familiale dating from 1953. Also visible are the rear direction indicator lamps, mounted above the rear wings on the D-pillars, and the stoneguards on the trailing edges of the front wings.

The 1953 models had new two-tone upholstery, as this picture of an 11 Légère shows.

Also new for 1953 was this dashboard, rather more deliberately styled than earlier types. In the centre is an ashtray, last seen on a Traction dashboard in 1934!

The 1953 11 Perfo engine, showing its characteristic short air filter.

The 11B Commerciale returned in April 1954, now with a single-piece tailgate and standard one-piece rear bumper.

A 1954 11D equipped as a taxi by the factory. Many pre-war Familiales also saw use as taxis after the war.

The light colour of this 1953 15-Six makes it possible to see the additional ventilator flaps below the headlamps which had been introduced in mid-1950.

For 1954, hubcaps were painted light grey around a chromed centre, as on this 11B Normale.

The 15-Six H was hard to distinguish from earlier six-cylinder cars without a look underneath. This is one of the very last.

The official "last-of-line" car was this 11 Normale. The date was 25th July 1957.

VARIATIONS

Despite the fact that its monocoque construction made major coachwork transformations a complicated business, the Traction Avant did inspire a few conversions in its early days. The robustness of its drivetrain attracted some manufacturers, who bought Citroën engines and other mechanical elements to install in their own vehicles, and others even bought Traction Avant bodyshells in order to give their own vehicles more modern styling in the 1930s.

After the War, however, the styling of the Traction Avant became dated much more quickly than its mechanical elements. As a result, bodywork transformations, both major and minor, increased in popularity. The car's continued popularity persuaded many accessory manufacturers to produce bolt-on accessories. And lastly, the Traction Avant was adopted as official transport by the French authorities, with the result that a number of special variants were created.

Special bodies

Relatively few special bodies appear to have been built for the Traction Avant before the 1939–1945 War, no doubt because monocoque technology was still very new and the traditional coachbuilders fought shy of tampering with the factory-developed product. Nevertheless, the AEAT coachwork company of Neuilly-sur-Seine offered a folding-roof conversion as early as 1935, and this remained available until the early 1950s. In general conception, this was not unlike the Salmons "Tickford" conversion offered in Britain in the 1930s. In Belgium and Holland, similar folding-roof conversions were supplied direct from the local Citroën assembly plants.

During the late 1940s, however, a large number of special bodies for the Traction Avant appeared on the market. One reason was that the styling was now beginning to look old-fashioned and that entrepreneurs saw their chance to make money by updating it; another was that greater experience of monocoque shells had given coachbuilders and engineers more confidence in their own ability to effect successful transformations; the absence from the post-War market of Citroën's own roadster had left a gap for open coachwork; and lastly, the seller's market in the late 1940s inspired many small companies to take risks which they might not have taken in more sober times by putting their designs into limited production.

It is impossible to provide accurate figures for the major bodywork conversions carried out on Traction Avant models during the late 1940s and early 1950s. In many cases, bodywork conversions offered by the smaller companies may have found no buyers, with the result that the prototype or demonstration model remained the only one of its kind. In other cases, coachbuilders were specially commissioned to build one-off bodies by wealthy clients. Major coachbuilders did produce some of their offerings in quantity, but the examples of the Swiss coachbuilders Worblaufen (15 cabriolet conversions in 1948–1949) and Langenthal (54 cabriolets in 1952–1953) show that large numbers were not involved. The demand was not only for open cars, of course: restyled saloons were also popular.

Commercial variants

Citroën's Danish importers in Copenhagen converted a number of Traction Avant saloons into vans in the late 1940s and early 1950s, to meet local demand created by tax regulations favourable to such vehicles. A very small number of saloons were also converted into vans or pick-up trucks by coachbuilders both small and large, but in most cases these were retrospective conversions of damaged or worn-out vehicles.

Bolt-on extras

Particularly in the 1940s and 1950s, a wide variety of bolt-on aftermarket accessories became available for the Traction Avant. Their scope ranged from small items like wheel embellishers and foglamps to four-speed gearboxes, restyled grilles and wings which were designed to update the appearance of the cars cheaply. Like items of their type in all eras, they were probably popular only briefly, and many were probably shoddily constructed.

Traction components in other cars

The sleek and low styling of the Traction Avant had an enormous impact on the car market in the mid-1930s, and other major French manufacturers sought to emulate or upstage it in their own ways. For the minor manufacturers, however, such radical transformations were out of the question for financial reasons and, in order to keep up, two of them actually purchased bare Traction Avant bodyshells from Citroën and adapted them to make their own vehicles.

Developing new front-wheel-drive mechanical elements would also have been prohibitively expensive, of course, and so both these companies actually mounted the Traction Avant bodyshells on to their existing rear-wheel-drive chassis! In this way, Delage produced its DI-12 model during 1936, and Licorne produced its Rivoli and Normandie models, each with a wide variety of engine options. None sold in large quantities, however.

The advanced technology incorporated into Maurice Sainturat's OHV wet-liner engine also attracted smaller manufacturers who needed to buy in drivetrain elements, and in some cases they also purchased the Citroën gearbox and other front-wheel-drive components. Notable among those who did so – mainly in the later 1930s – were Andreau, Chenard et Walker, Delage, Georges Irat, Licorne and Rosengart. Once again, production quantities were never large.

Official cars

The Traction Avant was bought in quantity by the French Army after 1947, and these official vehicles were always painted in the military's olive drab. When used in Algeria, they were fitted with 16-inch wheels and special tyres in order to give greater ground clearance and better traction on unmade roads. Some Tractions appear to have been fitted with armour plate and with machine guns for military use. As late as 1954, the French Army was still ordering both 11 Normale and 15-Six saloons, and the six-cylinder models remained in use as staff cars for senior military officers until the end of the decade.

The French Police, however, did not generally use the Traction Avant. It was the Parisian Police which became the exception when it acquired 350 examples between 1949 and 1951. The reason for this change of heart at such a late stage was that Paris was then suffering a crime wave at the hands of a gang of criminals who regularly used Tractions as getaway cars because they could out-handle and outrun the Renaults which were then standard Police issue! Many Police models were fitted with two-way radio equipment, with a generator in the boot; many also had special radiator grilles which concealed a siren mounted on the gearbox casing. After they were withdrawn from service, the Paris Police cars were returned to standard specification and sold in the French Colonies.

In the early 1950s, the six-cylinder Traction Avant had also become the official transport of French Government officials, and so it was no surprise that the President of the Republic, René Coty, should have ordered two further six-cylinder models as late as 1955. Both were specially coachbuilt for use on State occasions, and both were based on specially-built 15-Six Familiales with hydropneumatic suspension; the reason allegedly, is that Coty's doctor told him that this suspension would give maximum relief to his varicose vein problems!

Neither car bore the remotest resemblance to a standard Traction Avant, and both had the slab-sided lines typical of the mid-1950s. The first car was built as a six-light saloon by the coachbuilder Franay, to the design of Philippe Charbonneaux, and was displayed at the 1955 Paris Motor Show on the coachbuilder's stand. The second appeared in 1956 and was built as a cabriolet by Chapron, its most unusual feature being a sharp drop in the waistline just ahead of the rear passenger seat, which was intended to make the VIP travelling in the rear more visible to those outside. The saloon's main claim to fame was an unfortunate breakdown while on active service in 1957 with Her Majesty Queen Elizabeth II on board; the cabriolet remained in service until 1974.

Several companies offered folding-roof conversions of the Traction saloons, but the most popular was this one, introduced as early as 1935 by AEAT of Neuilly-sur-Seine. The company's initials stood for Anciens Etablissements Ansart et Teisseire. This 15-Six dating from the late 1940s also has the AEAT big-boot conversion, with the spare wheel still mounted externally.

More complete transformations became popular in the late 1940s. This 15-Six convertible was one of 15 built at Worblaufen in Switzerland by a small coachworks which named itself after the town.

This 1938 Slough-built car was rejuvenated by means of the New Look styling kit offered from 1948 by the New Service Station of Chiswick in London.

Another late 1930s model, this time French-built, rejuvenated by one of the add-on grilles which were available in the late 1940s. This one was made by the E.T. company of Courbevoie-sur-Seine.

Une des 530 fourgonnettes danoises spécialement transformées aux ateliers de Copenhague.

In Denmark, 530 of these vans were converted from saloons by the Citroën importers in Copenhagen.

The Licorne Normandie of 1937 used the bodyshell of an 11 Normale, bolted to a conventional chassis with rear-wheel drive. The more upright grille and traditional wings-and-running-boards styling do help to conceal the origins of the body.

The Franay-bodied Presidential car on the coachbuilder's stand at the 1955 Paris Motor Show. It was modified in 1959 and again in 1968, and remained in service until the end of 1970. The car still survives, in a private collection.

The Chapron-bodied Presidential parade car was delivered in 1956 and remained in service until 1974.

THE SLOUGH-BUILT TRACTION AVANT

Relatively few foreign cars were available on the British market when the Traction Avant was introduced to this country in September 1934. The main reason was that the Government of the time had introduced protectionist measures to safeguard domestic motor manufacturers in the wake of the Great Depression. Under these measures, cars sold in Britain had to have a high percentage of local content, and those which did not do so attracted high tax penalties. Similar policies were extended to cover cars sold in the Commonwealth, with the result that British manufacturers enjoyed a huge protected market for their products.

However, these new policies made little difference to Citroën, whose manufacturing subsidiary at Slough had been building cars for the British market and for certain export markets since 1926. By 1934, Citroën Cars Ltd was therefore accustomed to working with these policies, and needed only to organise manufacture of the Traction Avant so that the rules on local content were met. Broadly speaking, its solution was similar to the ones it had adopted for other Citroën models: it imported the essential elements of the car from France as a "kit" in component form, then sourced the additional elements locally and arranged for enough of the actual assembly to be done at Slough to meet the target percentage of manufacturing costs incorporated in the local-content regulations.

As a result, Citroën's Slough subsidiary became a major manufacturer and exporter of the Traction Avant. Beween 1934 and 1955, when production at Slough ended in favour of the DS, more than 25,000 Tractions were built in Britain. Although the vast majority had right-hand-drive, the Slough factory also built a few hundred left-hand-drive examples. Probably more than 50% of all those it made were exported, to Aden, Australia, Ceylon, Cyprus, Egypt, Gibraltar, Ghana, Hong Kong, India, Jamaica, Jordan, Kenya, Kuwait, Malaysia, Malta, Mauretania, Mozambique, New Zealand, Nigeria, Rhodesia, Singapore, South Africa, Sudan, Tanganyika, Uganda, the United States of America and Zambia. In addition, Slough-built cars were exported to Belgium, Holland and Switzerland when supplies from either the Paris or Brussels factories were insufficient to meet demand in those markets.

The tastes of the British market, and of those markets to which British manufacturers regularly exported, differed in several ways from those of the French market. As a result, the Slough-built Tractions differed in several important respects from their French equivalents. The most radical differences were always in the interior, where the seats were almost invariably upholstered in leather instead of cloth and the dashboard was faced with polished wood instead of finished in painted metal. However, there were dozens of other minor differences, mainly because Slough used British-made instead of French-made components in a number of areas in order to keep its local-content percentage up. In addition, the time-lag between supply of parts from France and their assembly into complete cars in Britain usually meant that new items would not appear on British-built cars until some months after their announcement in France.

Before looking in detail at the history of the Slough-built cars, it is worth making one further general point. Citroën's practice in France was to describe as "1935 models" only those cars built within the 1935 calendar-year, whereas Citroën Cars Ltd followed the British practice of opening its model-year at the Olympia Motor Show held the preceding October. Thus, a 1935-model Slough car could have been built at any time between October 1934 and September 1935 approximately, and a car built in October 1935 would have been a 1936 model!

The first Slough-built Tractions

Even before the Traction Avant was announced in Britain, there had been reports about it in the leading motoring journals, which had stressed the excellence of its road-holding. These reports were based on experience with French-built cars, of course, and in fact the first few Tractions sold in Britain were also French-built. They were equipped with a number of the British-made components which would later become standard on Slough-built cars, however, and it is probable that they had been imported primarily to allow fitting trials and for publicity or other demonstration purposes.

Production proper of the Traction Avant began at Slough in October 1934, and the first cars were "1935 models". Three types were available: saloon, roadster and fixed-head coupé (faux-cabriolet) versions of the 7CV, all with the 1,303cc engine which had just been superseded in France by the 1,628cc type. They were marketed under the name of "Super Modern Twelve".

The origin of that name is worth examination. Under the British RAC system of taxation, the 1,303cc engine was rated as a 12hp – hence the "Twelve". However, the Traction Avant was not the only Citroën 12hp being made at Slough, because the British factory would continue for a time to assemble rear-wheel-drive Rosalie models from parts already sent over from France. Faced with existing Light Twelve and Big Twelve models, Citroën Cars Ltd had to think of something different, and "Super Modern" seemed appropriate to describe the Traction Avant.

The Slough-built cars were easy to distinguish from their Paris-built sisters. Most obvious were two-piece vee-bumpers in place of the standard items with their graceful downward curve in the centre, and the windscreen wipers which were linked by a bar so that a single motor could operate both in tandem. On roadsters, the seat back was slightly further rearwards than on Paris-built cars, and so the hood cover had a distinctive cutout to allow for this. Leather upholstery and a generally more plush feel to the interior were also distinguishing features, although the wooden dashboard facings appear not to have been fitted to these first cars. They probably arrived towards the end of 1934.

The range was soon developed. In February 1935, the Super Modern Twelve took on the 1,628cc engine of the 7C models (which put its RAC rating up to 12,8hp), the 11 Légère appeared in saloon form as the "Sports Twelve" and the 11 Normale appeared as a saloon or seven-seater Familiale under the rather more realistic name of "Super Modern Fifteen". The 1,911cc engine of the French 11CVs was rated at 15hp under the RAC system, although it would be wrong to assume that Citroën Cars Ltd was trying to mislead the public by suggesting that the 15hp Sports Twelve was actually rated as a 12hp. It was in fact common practice for British manufacturers to use horsepower ratings in model-names to suggest the size of the car rather than the size of its engine, and by that way of reckoning an 11 Légère (Sports Twelve) was closer to a 7 (Super Modern Twelve) than it was to an 11 Normale (Super Modern Fifteen)!

At the Motor Show at Olympia in October 1935, Citroën Cars announced a number of further revisions. Most important was the opening luggage boot on saloons, which was announced at more or less the same time as its announcement on French-built cars. However, it is unlikely that models with this feature were actually available before the beginning of 1936, because Slough would have had to use up its supplies of old-style body shells first. Probably all the Slough-built cars with the opening boot had a distinguishing feature not found on French models: the boot lid could be supported in the open position by a pair of hinged arms, and a metal plate could be slid across it to form an extension of the boot floor so that extra luggage could be carried. It was a peculiarly British practice to build cars with a folding external luggage grid at the rear for just this purpose, and the modification had clearly been carried out to meet customer expectations.

The opening-boot cars also took on the steel roof panel standardised on French-built cars at the end of 1934, and both front and rear bumpers changed at this stage, becoming single-piece units with a small triangular ornament in the centre of the vee. The painted grille introduced on French-built cars in October 1935 replaced the chromed type, while its chevrons now came out from behind the bars. Inside, the only change was that a dash-lighting rheostat was added.

1936–1940: adding appeal
The names "Super Modern Twelve" and "Super Modern Fifteen" did not roll off the tongue too easily,

and it was probably for this reason that the Traction Avant range shown at the Olympia Show in October 1936 consisted of a plain Twelve, a plain Fifteen, and a Sports Twelve. The cars were basically the same as before, but Citroën Cars was clearly trying very hard to give the Traction additional appeal, no doubt because sales were slower than expected. All the signs confirm this: the Show witnessed home-market price reductions and revised specifications on Traction models, as well as the expansion of the range of Rosalie-based rear-wheel-drive models which Slough had continued to produce even though they were no longer being made in Paris.

Something clearly had gone wrong with Slough's sales estimates. The seven-seater Fifteen (11 Normale Familiale) introduced in 1935 no longer figured in home market sales catalogues, and in its place was a new rear-wheel-drive "Family Fifteen" derivative of the Rosalie models. Records show that the unused six-light Traction Avant shells hung around at Slough until a bulk order from South Africa in 1938 allowed the company to dispose of the last of them. Other bodyshells also hung around at Slough waiting for orders which would see them turned into complete cars, and some roadsters and coupés put on the road in the later 1930s actually had bodyshells which dated from much earlier. This was hardly surprising, as the two-door cars were very slow sellers in Slough's markets.

Some of the specification revisions introduced at the 1936 Olympia Show had of course been introduced by the Paris factory first, and were simply there because Slough was obliged to follow suit. More revealing, though, were some of the changes Slough made which did not parallel those made in Paris. Into the first category came the new dashboard with its instrumentation ahead of the driver; but only on Slough-built Twelves and Fifteens was there also a pair of round instruments in the centre of the dash to give the enthusiastic (or perhaps simply concerned) driver more information about what was going on under the bonnet. Chrome returned to the grille bars (which remained painted in France), and neater flat bumpers without the vee complemented a new style of Michelin wheels. Made in Britain, these had perforated rims to give a "spoked" effect, and were doubtless intended to appeal to the British motorist who was still largely attuned to spoked wire wheels. There were new paint colours, and the black wings obligatory since 1934 now disappeared, a few months before the same change was made on French-built cars. In addition, a sliding metal sunroof – a feature expected on equivalent British cars – was made standard.

The lower prices held until the 1937 Olympia Show, when those of the Twelves were increased, although the Fifteens were kept at their October 1936 levels. The Sports Twelve (11 Légère) was renamed a Light Fifteen, in a reversal of the 1935 decision, and the 1938 models had a new circular enamelled badge at the top left of their grilles, which bore the Citroën name in

Gothic letters – a most unfortunate choice at a time when the threat of war with Germany was looming ever larger! The only other change at the 1937 Show followed Parisian practice: the horns were repositioned and their grilles were deleted from the wings.

It looks as if sales did not pick up dramatically over the next twelve months. Citroën Cars resorted to drastic measures at the October 1938 Olympia Show. It announced budget-price "Popular Twelve" and "Popular Light Fifteen" models, which were right-hand-drive 1938-model Paris-built 7C and 11BL models with the traditionally French austere levels of trim. Presumably the plan was to reduce equipment levels on the Slough-built cars in due course if these "popular" models caught on; but they proved hard to sell and the plan, if such it was, fell through. Meanwhile, sales of the Twelve and Light Fifteen coupés had not proved enough to justify keeping them in the range beyond the date of their demise in France, and Slough no longer listed them.

October 1938 was also the date when Citroën Cars standardised Pilote wheels on its remaining models, some nine months behind Paris on this occasion. Unlike Paris, however, it continued to offer a wide range of colour schemes and therefore chose to paint the wheels in body-colour rather than in the red or yellow which Paris used to contrast with its almost-universal black paintwork. Also unlike Paris, Slough deleted the large chevrons from the radiator grille, replacing them with a small chevron badge mounted at the top left of the grille. Lastly, perhaps because the public had already done so, it renamed the Fifteen (11 Légère) as a "Big Fifteen", to distinguish it more readily from the Light Fifteen (11 Normale).

Further changes were made in the autumn of 1939, just before the outbreak of War. Once again a few months behind Paris, Citroën introduced the 7 Eco as a direct replacement for the Twelve (and retained the Twelve name for it), and fitted the uprated "Perfo" engines to the Light Fifteen and Big Fifteen. A Big Fifteen roadster was announced (Paris had been making an 11 Normale roadster since 1934), but only four or five were made before the War put an end to production. Clearly hoping to take the Traction up-market, the British subsidiary also announced an extra-cost Grand Luxe option for all models, which brought huge Lucas P80 headlamps, a pair of bumper-mounted foglamps, horns on either side of the grille and a more opulent three-piece wooden dashboard with a "Brooklands" spring-spoke steering wheel. Grilles on these cars were of course chromed, and also had large chevrons behind the vertical bars.

The most intriguing of the 1930 introductions, however, was the Slough-built 15-Six, which attracted the name of Citroën Six in its British-market version. Even the standard-equipment version was to be lavishly equipped by the standards of the Paris-built models in order to be competitive with British cars in the same price bracket. Thus, it was announced with folding central armrests in both front and rear seats, together with folding picnic tables in the rear of the front seat. On the Grand Luxe versions, a sunroof complemented the additions available on Grand Luxe versions of the Twelves and Fifteens. The War prevented the Six from going into full production, however; Citroën Cars allocated a block of 50 serial numbers for the new model, but probably no more than a handful were ever made. Only one – a Grand Luxe model – is known to survive, and that is currently in South Africa.

Wartime and after: 1940–1950

After the outbreak of War, it was obviously impossible for Paris to export any more Traction Avant "kits" to Slough, and the British factory simply built up its remaining stock into complete cars before ceasing car assembly for the duration. A few Twelve and Light Fifteen saloons were the only Tractions built at Slough during the hostilities, and it appears that all were exported to Commonwealth countries.

When the War ended, Citroën Cars was the only foreign manufacturer granted a licence to build vehicles in the United Kingdom, and its permit stipulated that the majority of those built must be exported. This was not a condition peculiar to Citroën, however: Government policies of the time encouraged all British manufacturers to build vehicles primarily for export, and threatened to curtail supplies of sheet steel (which were strictly rationed) to those which did not comply. As the 1940s wore on, the Government increased the "export quota", or percentage of vehicles in a manufacturer's output which had to be sold overseas, and Citroën Cars was subjected to the same set of requirements.

Before the War, Citroën Cars had exported only some 10% of its total production. That total now rose dramatically and, in the 20 years between the resumption of assembly at Slough in 1946 and the factory's closure in 1966, around 53% of all vehicles went for export. Traction production did not last throughout that period, of course, and gave way to assembly of the DS in 1955. Nevertheless, the overall balance was probably tipped even more heavily towards exports during the period when Slough was building Tractions.

The only model available from Slough when production recommenced in 1946 was the Light Fifteen (11 Légère) saloon, which came in either black or beige, in either case with beige upholstery, and was equipped with Pilote wheels. In all other respects except for the windscreen wipers mounted on the scuttle, it was identical to the model which had gone out of production in 1940. However, there is little doubt that in practice these first post-War cars had a wide variety of specifications, as Slough struggled to produce cars with whatever parts it could lay its hands on. The situation was no better by the autumn of 1946, and the 1947-model Tractions seem to have suffered from the same lack of a standard specification.

Assembly built up slowly, but as the materials supply situation began to ease, a standard specification did emerge. On 1948 models, the large chevrons returned to the grille (although they were now behind it rather than in front) and new curved bumper blades were fitted. Also distinctively British were perforated Rubery Owen wheels with a push-on hubcap, which replaced the Pilotes fitted to most 1946–1947 models.

It was probably increasing sales success which prompted Citroën Cars Ltd to reintroduce the Six at the 1948 Motor Show – Britain's first since the War. Unfortunately, the car did not come with the very high levels of equipment which had been offered on its 1940-model British equivalent; Slough had put the emphasis more on the car's spaciousness (it came as a full six-seater with a bench front seat) and performance levels. Options could be had, of course: like the Light Fifteen, the Six could be bought with a Weathershields sliding sun roof. And right from the beginning, Citroën had made sure that the Six was visually distinctive by giving it heavier round-section bumpers than the Light Fifteen and a large "6" on the cover plate for the starting handle aperture in the grille.

Only a small number of Sixes came off the lines at Slough before the end of 1948, and the car did not become available in practice until the early months of 1949. Sales in its first year were encouraging, but it was already obvious that it would never become a really strong seller. In Britain, its excellent main-road performance was seen as insufficient compensation for its fearsomely heavy steering at low speeds, and those who wanted six seats were generally content with the less spacious interiors of the latest saloons from domestic manufacturers.

Over the next few years, sales of the Slough-built Traction Avant took repeated knocks from these new saloons. The first impact came in 1949, when the new models introduced at the 1948 Earls Court Motor Show – Britain's first since the War – became more generally available in the markets where Slough was selling its Tractions. A slight recovery during 1950 did not affect the downward trend, for it was at the Earls Court Motor Show that autumn that Ford introduced its new Zephyr Six, a bargain-priced six-cylinder model with modern styling which undercut the Light Fifteen by a huge margin. During 1951, Light Fifteen sales took a battering and, although improvements to the Tractions in 1952 helped sales to improve again, a further downturn in 1954 spelled the end for the Traction at Slough. The DS arrived only just in time in mid-1955.

Meanwhile, 1949 had seen Slough start to build left-hand-drive cars for the first time, these being Light Fifteens which were mainly intended to supplement production shortfalls in the Paris and Brussels factories. In 1951, Light Fifteens had gained overriders and a stylised wing badge to cover the starting handle cutout in the grille. The finger-tip control stalk for horns and lights had been changed for the type already found on French-built cars, and the door trims had been extensively revised to incorporate map pockets, wooden garnish rails, and carpeted kick-panels.

Just as in France, 1952 was the year of the big-boot models, and these were announced in September, as usual a few months behind production in Paris. At the same time, the heater control was moved to the dashboard, which also acquired an ignition advance-and-retard lever to allow for the gradual improvements in the quality of petrol now that post-War austerity was almost over. A two-spoke steering wheel replaced the three-spoke type, and there was a pneumatic self-cancelling switch for the semaphore indicators. New rear lamps were fitted to the wings, with tail and stop lights incorporated within the same housing, and there was also a new type of exhaust silencer. On the Six, footrests were now supplied for the rear passengers.

These footrests and the bench front seat were also supplied as standard in a model new to post-War Britain, the Big Fifteen. A Big Fifteen had of course been available in 1939, but Slough had seen no need for it in the late 1940s, when the Light Fifteen seemed able to take care of the medium-saloon market and the Six was available for those who wanted a larger car. The relative failure of the Six was probably what prompted Slough to reintroduce the Big Fifteen, for the car was as roomy as a Six but cheaper to buy and more economical to run. Production figures from Slough suggest that a pair of pilot-build examples had been made during 1951, but production proper did not of course begin until autumn 1952. Sales during the remaining months of 1952 were not strong, but over the next few years sales did improve and it was clear that the Big Fifteen had taken the lion's share of the former market for the Six.

There were no significant changes for 1953 at Slough, not least because that was the year when the British factory began to assemble 2CV models and a great deal of time had to be devoted to the installation of the new production line. That year also saw the last few left-hand-drive Light Fifteens come off the assembly lines at Slough. The main news for 1954 was that Michelin X radial tyres became available for the first time in Britain (they had been available since 1948 in France) and were fitted as standard to Slough-built Tractions. The Six took on an attractive new dashboard with two round dials, which was quite different from anything ever seen on French models, but the Light Fifteen and Big Fifteen remained unchanged.

It never was quite clear what Citroën Cars Ltd intended to call the 15-Six H when it went on sale in Britain, and road tests referred to it by the rather cumbersome name of Six (Hydro-pneumatic). The car featured on the Citroën stand at the Earls Court Motor Show in October 1954, but only two examples appear to have been built that year. Production of the standard Six ceased at Slough, and all the 1955 six-cylinder cars built in Britain had the hydropneumatic rear suspension. That year was also notable for the use of plastic instead of cloth for the headlining of both Light and Big Fifteen models, and for the construction of a batch of 25 six-window Big Fifteens. These cars, of which 24 were Familiales and one a Commerciale, were constructed to special order for Australia, and were the only six-window cars to be made at Slough after 1938.

The DS was introduced to the French public at the 1955 Paris Motor Show, which opened at the beginning of October, and it went on display at the Earls Court Show which opened nearly three weeks later, alongside a Light Fifteen, a Big Fifteen and a 2CV. The six-cylinder Traction Avant was no longer in the British range (although a few cars may still have remained unsold), and the Light and Big Fifteens which were sold after the Motor Show were old-stock models. As 1955 turned into 1956, the DS took over, and a new chapter in the history of Citroën Cars Ltd began.

A familiar picture of a car which must be familiar to all British Traction enthusiasts: the 1938 Slough-built faux-cabriolet belonging to Fred Annells.

This picture of a late 1940s model, taken from sales literature of the time, shows some of the Slough characteristics. The grille is all chrome, there are Rubery Owen wheels, bumpers are quite different from their French equivalents, there are sidelights on the front wing crowns and the door handles are straight instead of curly. In addition, windscreen wipers are mounted at the base of the screen (long before this was so on French-built cars) and there are semaphore trafficators in the tops of the centre pillars.

Slough did produce some strange hybrids, however. This Light Fifteen, registered in 1950, has the French style of door handles and front bumper, but all other elements seem to be to Slough specifications.

Also to an unusual specification is this 1954 Slough car, with the Pilote wheels which had ceased to be standard wear in 1948. The sliding sunroof fitted to many Slough-built cars is shown in the open position.

A very clean 1953 Light Fifteen, fitted with the front window wind deflectors which Slough offered. Front overriders are missing on this example.

Under the bonnet of a Slough-built Light Fifteen. The washer bottle has been added to meet British traffic regulations.

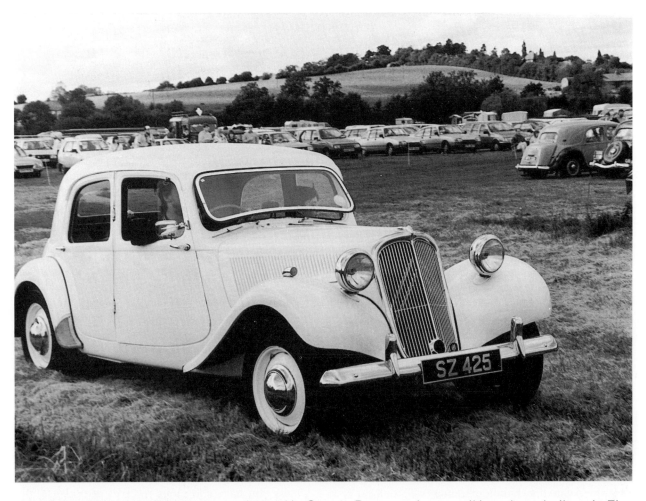

This 1955-model Light Fifteen was registered in County Down, and may well have been built up in Eire from CKD components sent out from Slough.

B U Y I N G ,   M A I N T A I N I N G   A N D   E N J O Y I N G   A
T R A C T I O N   A V A N T   T O D A Y

Although it would probably be rather eccentric to drive a Traction Avant as an everyday car in the 1990s, it would not be an impossibility. The Traction's longstanding popularity in the old-car movement means that spares and servicing expertise are readily available, while further support is available from several thriving clubs in Europe and elsewhere.

But would you want to use a Traction Avant on a regular basis? For those accustomed to more modern machinery, the car's biggest drawback is surely its servicing requirements. The average modern car needs a service every 12,000 miles, but a Traction demands attention in the form of greasing every 600 miles – 20 times as often! Then, would you really want to look after a Traction yourself, or are you the sort of person who prefers to give the car to a garage when things go wrong? No problem if you are, but remember that the mechanics at your local garage will probably never have seen a Traction before, and they could well inadvertently damage something through ignorance. To get work done properly, you will need to take the car to one of the specialists. There are several of them, but do not expect to find one on your doorstep.

Then there is the question of the car's driveability. A Traction Avant may handle extremely well for a car of its age, but it will not be able to keep up with modern machinery. You might find long motorway runs rather tiring, and you will probably not enjoy the car's heavy steering at parking speeds, the blind spots which make it awkward to park in restricted spaces, its poor (by modern standards) heating and ventilating arrangements, its typically Gallic gearchange, and its almost total lack of convenience features. However, it may be that none of these drawbacks deters you, and that you are simply seduced by the charm of the thing. If so, you have the makings of a true Traction enthusiast. Confirm your leanings by going along to some owners' club events (contact addresses are given later), and talk to existing owners to get a feel for the joys and pitfalls of ownership. The next thing to do is to set about finding a car.

Where to look

Even though there is no shortage of Tractions around today, you are very unlikely to find one advertised for sale in your local newspaper. Your best bet is to scan the advertisements in the classic car press, but even then you will not always find very many on offer. Most of the good examples have found long-term homes, and even the mediocre ones are mostly being restored these days. However, dealers do occasionally offer a Traction or two for sale; and many of the Traction spares and service specialists keep a small stock of cars which they are prepared to pass on. Otherwise, the best

source of information about cars for sale is the owners' clubs.

Some enterprising individuals have actually gone across to France to find the Traction of their dreams, and in some cases they have been successful. However, it is important not to run away with the idea that there are hundreds of well-preserved Tractions sitting around undiscovered in barns in rural France. The plain fact is that most of the good ones have already been found, and the rest are likely to be in a mess. Unfortunately, the average Frenchman who owned a Traction in the 1960s treated it like an old banger, and if he eventually put it away in a barn, it was because something serious had occurred which prevented it from carrying him from A to B. And naturally, French Tractions all have left-hand-drive.

The next thing to remember is that it is better not to set your heart on one particular variety of Traction, because the chances are that you will spend years searching for the right example. Original 7A models are rarer then hen's teeth nowadays; roadsters and cabriolets hardly ever change hands; and six-cylinder cars are not all that easy to find. Slough-built right-hand-drive cars, too, can be hard to track down. Unless you have enormous reserves of patience, the best thing is to resign yourself to ownership of the best French-built 11 Légère or 11 Normale you can find. These cars embody the essential character of the Traction better than any other, and there are plenty of them around.

What to look for

The crucial element in a Traction Avant is its monocoque bodyshell. It *is* strong when in good condition, but it is obviously not as strong if it has been weakened by rust. Unfortunately, rust does take hold only too often. It was not until the 1970s that car manufacturers started taking rust prevention seriously, and Citroën simply never thought about it when the Traction was in production between 1934 and 1957.

The first place to look for problems is in the body sills, which run along the sides of the car below the doors. Just ahead of the rear wheels, these sills have openings which allow access to the rear torsion bar adjusters, but which also allow mud and water into the hollow sill where they can set up rusting. By the time rust is visible on the outside of the sill, it is already serious. All cars with semaphore turn indicators (which means all the Slough-built models) are likely to suffer particularly badly, because rainwater gets past the indicator arms at the top of the central body pillars and runs down into the hollow sils, where it sets up further rusting from the inside.

If rust is not apparent in the sills, check that the

doors close properly. Sills weakened by rust will allow the body to sag in the middle, and this is most obvious if the doors scuff as they close. The most revealing areas are the trailing edges of the rear doors. Doors which do not close properly tend to put a strain on their hinges, and so a check of these is also advisable.

Cars which do have serious rot in the sills are not automatically write-offs, because the sills can be rebuilt. However, the job is time-consuming and expensive, and definitely not one for an amateur welder. The main consideration is really that cars with rotten sills are likely to have other problems as well, and that the total restoration bill is therefore likely to be high. How much you want to spend is entirely up to you, but you should make a sensible assessment based on the going price for a good example of the car you are looking at when you start your search. Be warned, however, that a full restoration of any car will almost always exceed the car's actual value.

The sills are of course not the only area of the all-steel bodyshell which suffers from rust. You will probably find more in the guttering, in the front wings, and in the boot floor. Here, look carefully at the area around the hinges on those cars with opening boots, because the weight of the boot lid can tear the hinges out of metal which has been weakened by rust. Inside the car, you should also check the floorpan, both at the edges where it adjoins the rust-prone sills and at the front underneath the scuttle ventilator, which is notorious for letting in water which eventually sets up rusting in the floor.

Doors also deserve a careful examination. Rainwater tends to run down inside them, and in a good car will escape through drain holes in the bottom face of the inner door panel. However, these drain holes tend to become blocked unless they are periodically cleared out, with the result that the rainwater stays inside the door and starts to rot through the steel panel. A line of bubbles along the bottom edge of the door will be the obvious sign that this has occurred. Replacement of the door skin might not be the only work necessary; sometimes, the inner panel will need repairs as well. Many Slough-built cars had a sliding sunroof, and the drain tubes for this tend to block, allowing water to stand in the roof channels and rot them through. Perished tubes can also allow water to rot through the metal windscreen pillars from the inside.

Have a look at the front bulkhead, too, because leaking battery acid can set up corrosion in this area. Lastly, check the condition of the front arms. Badly-repaired collision damage should be immediately apparent, and it is worth remembering that the arms are triple-skinned for strength, which also means that they are three times as difficult to repair as a single-skinned section if they have rusted. Collision damage could have caused rust to start almost anywhere in the arms, but you should check particularly for rust around the mountings for the steering rack and in the area where the steering column goes through the arm.

Moving on from the bodyshell, you need to assess the car's mechanical condition. The good news is that the wet-liner engines are long-lived and can be fairly readily rebuilt; most experts recommend fitting new piston and liner sets rather than reboring when cylinder wear becomes excessive. However, the white-metal bearings can wear after high mileages, and remetalling bearings is a costly job these days. For this reason, many owners have replaced early 1,911cc engines with the later 11D type, which has white metal main bearings but shell-type big ends, and is correspondingly more durable and easier to repair.

However, the cars' mechanical Achilles heel is its transmission, which was designed when front-wheel-drive was in its infancy and never benefited from the reliability of modern front-wheel-drive systems. Starting with the gearbox itself, the phosphor-bronze bushes on second and third gears tend to wear, leading to synchromesh problems and in bad cases to a tendency for the box to jump out of gear. When driving a Traction, listen for a howling noise from the front end: this is caused by worn teeth on the pinion gears in the final drive unit. In bad cases (often caused by regular bump-starting or tow starting of the car), these teeth can actually strip off the pinion gears.

Driveshafts are another weakness, and should be checked carefully. Only on late cars do they have protective leather gaiters, and without these they are subjected to bombardment from mud and grit thrown up from the road; split gaiters of course are as useless as no gaiters, because they allow road debris to attack the driveshafts and cause premature wear. However, even when properly treated, the driveshafts do not last long. Their inner joints are good for only about 15,000 miles, and those at the gearbox end are usually due for replacement after about 60,000 miles.

Wear mostly occurs in the bushing of the double Hooke joints in the driveshafts, and is accelerated if regular greasing (every 600 miles) is not carried out. Each driveshaft has two grease nipples for this purpose. When the car is on the move, a rhythmic knocking noise from the front end which gets louder as the vehicle is cornering will suggest worn driveshaft joints. You can confirm your suspicions when the car is stationary by grasping each end of the shaft firmly and twisting them in opposite directions. Wear will show up as excessive movement in the joint. Some owners have sacrificed originality for peace of mind by fitting driveshafts with modern CV joints. This is not a cheap conversion, but it is a sensible and practical one, and is becoming more and more common on cars which have been cared for by enthusiasts.

Most cars had a rack-and-pinion steering system (the exceptions were built before 1936 and are therefore very rare today). Like the driveshafts, this should be protected by rubber gaiters, and split gaiters can lead to premature wear. Replacement of these gaiters is time-consuming. Wear in the rack itself can be taken up to a certain extent by shimming, but you should also look for worn pins in the inner ball joints which transmit steering movement to the track rods. Front suspension and steering components need greasing as regularly as the driveshafts, and lack of attention here leads to wear in the upper swivel link ball joints and in the pins of the upper link arms. Worn Silentbloc rubber bushes in the front suspension may be the cause if there is serious judder as the car moves away from rest, but the same symptoms could indicate nothing more than a worn clutch plate.

During checks of other areas, you will probably by this stage already have formed an opinion about the state of the car's interior. Headlinings are often stained, either by cigarette smoke or by water (and in the latter case, you should try to find out where the water has come from), and can of course be replaced – at some cost. Reupholstery of the seats and door trims is also possible, but remember that Slough-built cars had leather upholstery (and even leather door trims up to 1937), and that replacement could prove very expensive. Slough-built cars also had wooden dashboards, which can deteriorate more than the plain metal type on other models.

Finally, check for electrical malfunctions. The Traction's electrical system is fortunately relatively simple, and so faults are easy to trace and not usually hard to cure. However, it is important to remember that all French-built cars had a six-volt system without fuses, while Slough-built cars had the more familiar 12-volt type. The fuses in the Slough system were unfortunately of minimal value – one covered the interior light while the second covered the wipers, brake lights and semaphore arms – and the system is really no safer than the French type because the main consumers of current are not fused. Elements of the six-bolt and twelve-volt systems – and that includes light bulbs – are not interchangeable. Some owners have converted six-volt cars to 12-volt electrics, but the only way to do this safely is to rewire the whole car and to add in a fuse box. Check, therefore, that a conversion has been properly done.

Support

Once you have bought your Traction, you will undoubtedly want to meet fellow-enthusiasts. In Great Britain, you should not hesitate to join either the Traction Owners' Club (2 Appleby Gardens, Dunstable, Bedfordshire LU6 3DB) or the all-model Citroën Car Club (P.O. Box 348, Bromley BR2 8QT). Contact addresses do change from time to time, and although those given were correct at the time of writing in 1993, you should double-check in the classic car magazines. These clubs get together with Traction enthusiasts' clubs from all over the world, and are a valuable source of knowledge, sympathy and camaraderie. In particular, the Traction Owners' Club keeps tabs on parts re-manufacturing programmes both in this country and abroad, and can point you in the right direction if you need an elusive spare.

Further reading will be a problem unless you can read French. Michael Sedgwick's small volume, *The Traction Avant Citroëns, 1934–1955* (Profile Publications, number 95), has unfortunately been out of print for many years, and the only other English-language publication devoted solely to the Traction is Brooklands Books' *Citroën Traction Avant Gold Portfolio, 1934–1957*, a fascinating collection of road tests and other articles about the cars.

If you can read French, Olivier de Serres' *Le Grand Livre de la Traction Avant* (published by EPA) is indispensable, although it is now hard to find and expensive. More readily available is the colourful *22 . . . V'la les Traction!* by Fabien Sabatès (published by Massin), and collections of French-language road tests and other articles about the cars taken from magazines can be found in Volumes 3 and 5 of the Collection Auto Archives series (published by Edition Nationale 7).

You can't beat
CITROEN
in the long run!

For Sale! This could be the start of serious temptation . . .

A different sort of temptation. Seen in a French field, this Traction sports one of the accessory grilles which were popular in the late 1940s, and early 1950s. But is it too far gone to restore?

Tractions abound in French scrapyards. This one dates from around 1954, and could yield useful spares. It is unlikely to be economically viable as a restoration project, however.

A successful import, now re-registered with a British number which reflects the date of its arrival in the UK.

APPENDIX   A

Specifications

7A

Models available: Saloon, Roadster and Faux-Cabriolet (May–June 1934).
Engine: 4-cyl., 72mm x 80mm, 1,303cc OHV. Compression ratio 5.7:1. Three-bearing crankshaft, Solex 30FV (later 30BFHD and 30THD) carburettor. 32bhp at 3,500rpm. French fiscal rating: 7CV.
Transmission: Three-speed; no synchromesh on first. Final drive 3.875:1.
Steering, suspension and brakes: Worm and roller steering. Independent front suspension by wishbones and torsion bars; dead rear axle with torsion bars; friction dampers. Hydraulic drum brakes all round.
Dimensions: Wheelbase 2.91 metres. Track 1.34 metres. Length 4.45 metres. Width 1.68 metres. Height 1.54 metres.

7B

Models available: Saloon, Roadster, Faux-Cabriolet, "Concours d'élégance" saloon and Cabriolet (June–October 1934).
Engine: 4-cyl., 78mm x 80mm, 1,529cc OHV. Compression ratio 5.7:1. Three-bearing crankshaft, Solex HBFD or BFHD carburettor. 35bhp at 3,200rpm. French fiscal rating: 9CV.
Transmission: Three-speed, no synchromesh on first. Final drive 3.875:1, or optional 4.375:1.
Steering, suspension and brakes: Worm and roller steering. Independent front suspension by wishbones and torsion bars; dead rear axle with torsion bars; friction dampers. Hydraulic drum brakes all round.
Dimensions: Wheelbase 2.91 metres. Track 1.34 metres. Length 4.45 metres. Width 1.68 metres. Height 1.54 metres. Weight 900kg.

7C

Models available: Saloon, Roadster (October 1934–February 1939) and Faux-Cabriolet (October 1934–September 1938).
Engine: 4-cyl., 72mm x 100mm, 1,628cc OHV. Compression ratio 5.9:1. Three-bearing crankshaft, Solex 30THD (or optional 30HTD) carburettor (type 30DHT from January 1938). 36bhp at 3,800rpm. French fiscal rating: 9CV.
Transmission: Three-speed, no synchromesh on first. Final drive 3,875:1, or optional 4.375:1 (to December 1937); 3.44:1 from January 1938.
Steering, suspension and brakes: Worm and roller steering (rack and pinion from May 1936). Independent front suspension by wishbones and torsion bars; dead rear axle with torsion bars; friction dampers (hydraulic telescopic dampers from May 1936). Hydraulic drum brakes all round. Pilote wheels from January 1938.
Dimensions: Wheelbase 2.91 metres. Track 1.34 metres. Length 4.45 metres. Width 1.68 metres. Height 1.54 metres. Weight 900kg.

7C Eco

Models available: Saloon (February 1939–June 1941).
Engine: 4-cyl., 72mm x 100mm, 1,628cc OHV. Compression ratio 6.2:1. Three-bearing crankshaft, Solex 30 ATHD carburettor. 36bhp at 3,800rpm. French fiscal rating: 9CV.
Transmission: Three-speed, no synchromesh on first. Final drive 3.1:1.
Steering, suspension and brakes: Rack and pinion steering. Independent front suspension by wishbones and torsion bars; dead rear axle with torsion bars; hydraulic telescopic dampers. Hydraulic drum brakes all round.
Dimensions: Wheelbase 2.91 metres. Track 1.34 metres. Length 4.45 metres. Width 1.68 metres. Height 1.54 metres. Weight 900kg.

7S

Models available: Saloon, Roadster and Faux-Cabriolet (June–November 1934).
Engine: 4-cyl., 78mm x 100mm, 1,911cc OHV. Compression ratio 5.9:1. Three-bearing crankshaft, Solex 30BFHD carburettor. 46bhp at 3,800rpm. French fiscal rating: 11CV.
Transmission: Three-speed, no synchromesh on first. Final drive 3.44:1.
Steering, suspension and brakes: Worm and roller steering. Independent front suspension by wishbones and torsion bars; dead rear axle with torsion bars; friction dampers. Hydraulic drum brakes all round. Michelin Super-Confort 150 x 40 tyres.
Dimensions: Wheelbase 2.91 metres. Track 1.34 metres. Length 4.45 metres. Width 1.68 metres. Height 1.54 metres. Weight 1,025kg.

11A ("Normale")

Models available: Saloon, Roadster, Faux-Cabriolet, Limousine, Familiale, Coupé Limousine (September 1934–January 1937) and Coupé de Ville (September 1934–December 1935).
Engine: 4-cyl., 78mm x 100mm, 1,911cc OHV. Compression ratio 5.9:1. Three-bearing crankshaft, Solex 30 THD carburettor. 46bhp at 3,800rpm.
Transmission: Three-speed, no synchromesh on first. Final drive 3.44:1.
Steering, suspension and brakes: Worm and roller steering (rack and pinion from May 1936). Independent front suspension by wishbones and torsion bars; dead rear axle with torsion bars; friction dampers (hydraulic

telescopic dampers from May 1936). Hydraulic drum brakes all round. Michelin Super-Confort 150 x 40 tyres (standard) or 160 x 40 (long-wheelbase).
Dimensions: Wheelbase 3.09 metres (standard) or 3.27 metres (long wheelbase). Front track 1.46 metres. Rear track 1.45 metres. Length 4.65 metres (standard) or 4.85 metres (long wheelbase). Width 1.76 metres. Height 1.54 metres. Weight 1,100kg.

11AL ("Légère")
Models available: Saloon, Roadster and Faux-Cabriolet (October 1934–January 1937).
Engine: 4-cyl., 78mm x 100mm, 1,911cc OHV. Compression ratio 5.9:1. Three-bearing crankshaft, Solex 30 THD carburettor. 46bhp at 3,800rpm.
Transmission: Three-speed, no synchromesh on first. Final drive 3.44:1.
Steering, suspension and brakes: Worm and roller steering (rack and pinion from May 1936). Independent front suspension by wishbones and torsion bars; dead rear axle with torsion bars; friction dampers (hydraulic telescopic dampers from May 1936). Hydraulic drum brakes all round. 150 x 40 tyres.
Dimensions: Wheelbase 2.91 metres. Track 1.34 metres. Length 4.45 metres. Width 1.68 metres. Height 1.54 metres. Weight 1,060kg.

11B ("Normale")
Models available: Saloon, Roadster, Familiale and Limousine (February 1937–March 1939), Faux-Cabriolet (February 1937–September 1938), Commerciale (March 1938–March 1939).
Engine: 4-cyl., 78mm x 100mm, 1,911cc OHV. Compression ratio 5.9:1. Three-bearing crankshaft, Solex 30 THD carburettor (30 DHT from January 1938). 46bhp at 3,800rpm.
Transmission: Three-speed, no synchromesh on first. Final drive 3.44:1. (3.875:1 with standard wheelbase and 3.44:1 with long wheelbase from January 1938; 3.875:1 on Commerciales).
Steering, suspension and brakes: Rack and pinion steering. Independent front suspension by wishbones and torsion bars; dead rear axle with torsion bars; hydraulic telescopic dampers. Hydraulic drum brakes all round. Michelin Super-Confort 150 x 40 tyres (standard) or 160 x 40 (long wheelbase). Pilote wheels with 165 x 400 tyres (standard wheelbase) or 185 x 400 (long wheelbase) tyres from January 1938.
Dimensions: Wheelbase 3.09 metres (standard) or 3.27 metres (long wheelbase). Track 1.46 metres (1.49 metres from January 1938). Length 4.65 metres (standard) or 4.85 metres (long wheelbase). Width 1.76 metres (1.79 metres from January 1938). Height 1.54 metres (1.56 metres from January 1938). Weight 1,100kg (from January 1938: 1,120kg for saloons, 1,180kg for Familiales, 1,210kg for Commerciales).

11BL ("Légère")
Models available: Saloon, Roadster (February 1937–

March 1939) and Faux-Cabriolet (February 1937–September 1938).
Engine: 4-cyl., 78mm x 100mm, 1,911cc OHV. Compression ratio 5.9:1. Three-bearing crankshaft, Solex 30 THD carburettor (30 DHT from January 1938). 46bhp at 3,800rpm.
Transmission: Three-speed, no synchromesh on first. Final drive 3.44:1 (3.875:1 from January 1938).
Steering, suspension and brakes: Rack and pinion steering. Independent front suspension by wishbones and torsion bars; dead rear axle with torsion bars; hydraulic telescopic dampers. Hydraulic drum brakes all round. 150 x 40 tyres, or 160 x 40 on long-wheelbase models. Pilote wheels with 165 x 400 tyres from January 1938.
Dimensions: Wheelbase 2.91 metres. Track 1.34 metres (1.37 metres from January 1938). Length 4.38 metres. Width 1.67 metres. Height 1.54 metres (1.52 metres from January 1938). Weight 1,060kg (1,070kg from January 1938).

11B Perfo ("Normale")
Models avaiable: Saloon (March 1939–February 1942 approx., March 1947–July 1957); Familiale (March 1939–February 1942 approx., July 1953–July 1957); Commerciale (March 1939–February 1942 approx., April 1954–July 1957); Roadster and Limousine (March–December 1939).
Engine: 4-cyl., 78mm x 100mm, 1,911cc OHV. Compression ratio 6.2:1 (6.5:1 from February 1950; 6.8:1 from May 1955). Three-bearing crankshaft, Solex 35 FATIP (later 35 FPAI) carburettor; type 32 PBIC from February 1950 (some cars with Zenith 32 IN carburettors in August 1950). 56bhp at 3,800rpm (57–59bhp at 4,000rpm from January 1953; 60bhp at 4,000rpm from May 1955).
Transmission: Three-speed, no synchromesh on first. Final drive 3.875:1 (standard wheelbase) or 3.44:1 (long wheelbase).
Steering, supension and brakes: Rack and pinion steering. Independent front suspension by wishbones and torsion bars; dead rear axle with torsion bars; hydraulic telescopic dampers. Hydraulic drum brakes all round.
Dimensions: Wheelbase 3.09 metres (standard) or 3.27 metres (long wheelbase). Track 1.47 metres. Length 4.65 metres (standard) or 4.85 metres (long wheelbase). Width 1.79 metres. Height 1.56 metres. Weight 1,120kg (saloons), 1,180kg (Familiales), 1,210kg (Commerciales).

11BL Perfo ("Légère")
Models available: Saloon (March 1939–June 1942, June 1945–July 1957) and Roadster (March–December 1939).
Engine: 4-cyl., 78mm x 100mm, 1,911cc OHV. Compression ratio 6.2:1 (6.5:1 from February 1950; 6.8:1 from May 1955). Three-bearing crankshaft, Solex 35 FATIP (later 35 FPAI) carburettor; type 32 PBIC from February 1950 (some cars with Zenith 32 IN car-

burettors in August 1950). 56bhp at 3,800rpm (57–59bhp at 4,000rpm from January 1953; 60bhp at 4,000rpm from May 1955).
Transmission: Three-speed, no synchromesh on first. Final drive 3.875:1.
Steering, suspension and brakes: Rack and pinion steering. Independent front suspension by wishbones and torsion bars; dead rear axle with torsion bars; hydraulic telescopic dampers. Hydraulic drum brakes all round.
Dimensions: Wheelbase 2.91 metres. Track 1.37 metres. Length 4.38 metres (4.45 metres from July 1952). Width 1.67 metres. Height 1.52 metres. Weight 1,070kg.

15 Six
Models available: Saloon (February 1939–February 1940; February 1946–January 1955), Familiale (March 1939–February 1940, September 1953–August 1955) and Limousine (March 1939–February 1940).
Engine: 6-cyl., 78mm x 100mm, 2,867cc OHV. Compression ratio 6.3:1 (6.2:1 from June 1947; 6.5:1 from January 1948). Four-bearing crankshaft, Solex 30 FFIAP 2 carburettor (Solex 30 PAAI from June 1947). 76bhp at 3,800rpm. French fiscal rating: 16CV.
Transmission: Three-speed, no synchromesh on first. Final drive 3.875:1. Single-plate clutch from June 1950.
Steering, suspension and brakes: Rack and pinion steering. Independent front suspension by wishbones and torsion bars; dead rear axle with torsion bars; hydraulic telescopic dampers. Hydraulic drum brakes all round. 185 x 400 tyres.
Dimensions: Wheelbase 3.087 metres (saloon). 3.27 metres (Familiale and Limousine). Track 1.48 metres. Length 4.76 metres (saloon), 4.96 metres (Familiale and Limousine). Width 1.79 metres. Height 1.56 metres. Weight 1,325kg (saloon), 1,339kg (Familiale and Limousine).

15 Six H
Models available: Saloon (April 1954–July 1956).
Engine: 6-cyl., 78mm x 100mm, 2,867cc OHV. Compression ratio 6.5:1. Four-bearing crankshaft, Solex 30 PAAI carburettor. 78–80bhp at 4,000rpm. French fiscal rating: 16CV.
Transmission: Three-speed, no synchromesh on first. Final drive 3.875:1. Single-plate clutch.
Steering, suspension and brakes: Front suspension by torsion bars with hydraulic dampers; self-levelling hydropneumatic rear suspension with swinging arms. Anti-roll bars front and rear. Hydraulic drum brakes. 165 x 400 tyres.
Dimensions: Wheelbase 3.087 metres (saloon), 3.27 metres (Familiale). Front and rear tracks 1.48 metres (saloon). Length 4.76 metres (saloon), 4.96 metres (Familiale). Width 1.79 metres (saloon). Height 1.56 metres (saloon). Weight 1,325kg (saloon), 1,339kg (Familiale).

Body styles

Commerciale:	six-light body on long wheelbase, with opening tailgate.
Coupé de Ville:	four-light saloon body on standard wheelbase, with division (available only on 11A, 1934–1935).
Coupé Limousine:	four-light body on long wheelbase, with panelled rear quarters. Also known as "Long coupé" or "Coupé de Ville".
Familiale:	six-light body on long wheelbase, with six seats and three forward-facing jump-seats behind the front bench. In 1934–1936, and then again from 1954, the 11 was available as a taxi, with a division incorporated in the nine-seater Familiale (or six-seater Limousine) body.
Faux-cabriolet:	two-door, three-seater closed coupé body on standard wheelbase.
Limousine:	six-light body on long wheelbase, with six seats.
Roadster:	two-door, three-seater open body on standard wheelbase, with convertible top and "dickey seat".
Saloon:	four-light body on standard wheelbase, with five/six seats.

A P P E N D I X   B

Serial numbers

The numbers given here are the first and last known numbers in each respective sequence. Not all numbers within a given sequence were used for the same models (e.g. 1934 7S models were numbered within the 7B sequence), and some numbers within some sequences were not used at all.

1934

7A	7B	7S	7C	11A	11AL
000001	010001	020001	050001	10000	350001
– 007000	– 030620	– 021500	– 056700	– 103300	– 351500

1935

			7C	11A	11AL
			056701	103301	351501
			– 071400	– 107700	– 353500

1936

			7C	11A	11AL
			071401	107701	353501
			– 093000	– 116600	– 358800

1937

	7C	11A	11AL	11AM
	093001	116601	358801	**360000**
	– 200001	– 204300	– 358840	– 360315
		11B		11BL
		118001		360501
		– 127300		– 38600

1938

	7C	11B	11 Comm	11BL	15-Six
	204301	127301	200000	386001	680000
	– 210500	– 139200	– 291200	– 422400	– 680090

1939

	7C/Eco	11B	11 Comm	11BL	15-Six
	210501	139201	291201	422401	680091
	– 218600	– 152350	– 292670	– 450000	– 682400

1940

	7 Eco	11B	11 Comm	11BL
	218601	152351	292671	450001
	– 219800	– 153300	– 293211	– 454500

1945

| | | 11BL | |
| | | 457600 | |

1946

		11BL	15-Six G
		457601	682479
		– 469600	– 683690

1947

	11B	11BL	15-Six G
	154770	469601	682691
	– 156600	– 488200	– 682729

			15-SixD
			682730
			– 682800

1948

	11B	11BL	15-Six D
	156601	488201	682801
	– 164000	– 508800	– 685500

1949

	11B	11BL	15-Six D
	163951	508801	685501
	– 177700	– 531500	– 691600

1950

	11B	11BL	15-Six D
	177701	531501	691601
	– 195500	– 556200	– 701600

1951

	11B	11BL	15-Six D
	195501	556201	701601
	– 212100	– 582200	– 713000

1952

	11B	11BL	15-Six D
	212101	582201	713001
	– 236600	– 612000	– 721650

1953

11B	11 Comm	11BL	15-Six D
236601	293593	612001	721651
– 270800		– 636900	– 723710

1954

11B	11 Comm	11BL	15-Six D	15-Six H
270801	295000	636901	723711	726001
– 299999	– 301000	– 652800	– 724950	– 727680

1955

	11B	11 Comm	11BL	15-Six D	15-Six H
	403601	301001	652801	724951	727681
	– 427300	– 304940	– 667400	– 725390	– 729062

1956

	11B	11 Comm	11BL
	427301	304941	667401
	– 441990	– 307180	– 675905

1957

	11B	11 Comm	11BL
	441991	307181	675906
	– 444600	– 307860	– 677500

Serial numbers of Slough-built cars

These figures are taken from Slough factory records. They are incomplete and their accuracy cannot be guaranteed!

i) 1934–1940

	Type		*First serial no.*	*Body symbol*
1935	7A	(Super Modern Twelve)	100000	
	11A	(Sports Twelve)	115501	
	11L	(Fifteen)	121501	
1936	7AL	(Twelve)	101351	
	11AL	(Fifteen)	115651	
1937	7C	(Twelve)	102001	
	11C	(Fifteen)	116001	
	11CL	(Light Fifteen)	122001	
1938	7C2	(Twelve)	102501	
	11C2	(Fifteen)	116101	
	11CL2	(Light Fifteen)	122201	
1939	7C3	(Twelve Saloon and Roadster)	103301	
	11C3	(Big Fifteen Saloon and Family Fifteen)	116201	
	11CL3	(Light Fifteen Saloon and Roadster)	122551	
1940	7CP	(Twelve Saloon, standard)	105001	VP
	7C4	(Twelve Saloon, De Luxe)	106001	BRV
		(Twelve Roadster)		RPV
	11C4	(Fifteen Saloon)	116501	BPVS
	11C4	(Fifteen Roadster)		BPVL*
	11C4	(Family Fifteen)		FPVF
	11CLP	(Light Fifteen Saloon, standard)	124001	VPS
	11CL4	(Light Fifteen, De Luxe)	125001	BPVS
		(Light Fifteen Roadster)		RPVS
	15C4	(Six)	118001†	BPVL

* This code may be mistaken for RPVL, which are the body code letters on one known Fifteen Roadster.

† The sole surviving Six has chassis number 118012, which suggests that at least 12 were built (see main text, Chapter 8, and Production Figures in Appendix C).

i) 1946–1955

	Type	Serial numbers	Body symbol
1946	Light Fifteen (RHD)	126001 – 127199	
1947	Light Fifteen (RHD)	127300 – 129037	
1948	Light Fifteen (RHD)	129038 – 131522	
	Six	118051 – 118057	
1949	Light Fifteen (RHD)	131523 – 133374	
	Light Fifteen (LHD)	135001 – 135068	
	Six	118058 – 118292	
1950	Light Fifteen (RHD)	133375 – 135000	
		136001 – 136337	
	Light Fifteen (LHD)	135069 – 135178	
	Six	118293 – 118662	
1951	Light Fifteen (RHD)	136338 – 138908	
	Light Fifteen (LHD)	135179 – 135275	
	Big Fifteen (11C)	116571 – 116572	BPVL
	Six	118663 – 118975	
1952	Light Fifteen (RHD)	9/520001 – 9/521244	
	Light Fifteen (LHD)	135276 – 135310	
	Big Fifteen (11C)	9/525001 – 9/525076	BPVL
	Six	9/527501 – 9/527629	
1953	Light Fifteen (RHD)	9/53001 – 9/531598	
	Light Fifteen (LHD)	135311 – 135317	
	Big Fifteen (11C)	9/535001 – 9/535428	BPVL
	Six	9/537501 – 9/537594	
1954	Light Fifteen (RHD)	9/531599 – 9/532569	
	Light Fifteen (LHD)	135318 – 135317	
	Big Fifteen	9/535429 – 9/535839	BPVL
	Six	9/537595 – 9/537623	
	Six (Hydropneumatic)	9/547001 – 9/547002	
1955	Light Fifteen (RHD)	9/550001 – 9/550717	
	Big Fifteen	9/555001 – 9/555111	BPVL
	Family Fifteen	9/557001 – 9/557025	FPVF
	Six (Hydropneumatic)	9/557501 – 9/557575	

A P P E N D I X   C

Production figures

	7A/7B/ 7S	7C	11AL	11BL	11A	11B	11 Comm	15-Six	15-Six H	Total
1934	20,998		1,908		5,052					27,958
1935		14,076	2,181		1,854					18,111
1936		19,550	4,453		6,423					30,426
1937		11,019		26,112		9,839	2			46,972
1938		6,245		36,526		12,018	1,189	90		56,068
1939		8,120		27,473		12,916	1,478	2,309		52,296
1940		1,133		4,415		1,863	542	25		7,978
1941		154		2,038		329	350			2,871
1942				3		1				4
****										
1945				1,525					1,525	
1946				10,931		1		203		11,135
1947				19,348		1,697		108		21,153
1948				20,091		7,425		2,731		30,247
1949				22,834		14,012		6,047		42,893
1950				24,586		16,959		9,400		50,945
1951				25,344		17,180		11,752		54,276
1952				29,463		23,298		8,376		61,137
1953				25,048		34,532		2,388		61,968
1954				15,922		27,959	2,460	1,104	1,679	49,124
1955				15,007		23,778	3,948	58	1,349	44,140
1956				8,372		14,596	2,164	1	49	25,182
1957				1,248		2,616	686		2	4,552
Total	20,998	60,297	6,634	316,286	13,329	221,019	12,819	44,592	3,079	*700,961*

Total 7CV	81,295	(all pre-War)	
Total 11 Légère	324,828	(105,109 pre-War and 219,719 post-War)	
Total 11 Normale	234,348	(50,295 pre-War and 184,053 post-War)	
Total 11 Commerciale	12,819	(3,561 pre-War and 9,258 post-War)	
Total 15-Six and 15-Six H	47,671	(2,424 pre-War and 45,247 post-War)	

These figures include Traction Avant models assembled at Citroën's overseas assembly plants in:

Belgium (Brussels – Forest)	1934–1956
Germany (Cologne)	1934–1935
Great Britain (Slough)	1934–1955
Italy (Milan)	1934–1935
Poland (Warsaw)	1934–1935

Production at Slough

N.B. *Pre-War records are incomplete, and figures in italics are estimates only; these also affect overall totals. These figures are based on those given in Malcolm Bobbitt's book,* The British Citroën, *but they are at variance with those given by the main authority (Oliver de Serres'* Le Grand Livre de la Traction Avant). *"Years" in these tables are calendar-years and do not equate to the British model-year.*

	Twelve	Light Fifteen	LHD Light Fifteen	Big Fifteen	Six Cyl	Six-H	Total
1935	*1,350*	*650*					*2,000*
1936	*650*	*350*					*1,000*
1937	500	300					800
1938	900	350					1,250
1939	*1,700*	*1,450*		*300*			*3,450*
1940	?	?			*50*		*50*
****							
1946		1,199					1,199
1947		1,838					1,838
1948		2,484			7		2,491
1949		1,852	68		235		2,155
1950		1,963	110		370		2,443
1951		571	97	2	313		983
1952		1,225	35	77	130		1,467
1953		1,599	7	428	95		2,129
1954		971		411	29	2	1,413
1955		716		110		74	900
Total	*5,100*	*17,518*	317	*1,328*	1,229	76	*25,568*

For comparison, the totals given by de Serres are:

Twelve:	approx.	4,500	
Light Fifteen:	approx.	18,700	(including LHD)
Big Fifteen:	approx.	1,900	
Six Cyl.:	approx.	1,300	(including Hydropneumatic)
Total:	approx.	26,400	

A P P E N D I X   D

Performance figures

Note: These figures are approximations, and are given for guidance only. Exact figures vary quite widely from car to car.

Type	0–50mph	Max. speed	Standing ¼-mile	Fuel cons
7A (1303cc)	N/A	59 mph	N/A	N/A
7B (1529cc)	N/A	62 mph	N/A	N/A
7C (1628cc)	25 secs	63 mph	27 secs	24–32 mpg
11 Légère	15 secs	77 mph	23 secs	23 mpg
11 Normale	23 secs	72 mph	25 secs	21 mpg
15-Six	12.5 secs	84 mph	21.5 secs	19 mpg

A P P E N D I X   E

Colour Schemes

Note: Experts disagree on the full range of colours applied on the production lines in Paris, and this list cannot therefore be considered definitive. Names are given in English, and their French equivalents are provided at the end of the list. The list does not include the special colours applied by importers and dealers to cars shipped overseas in primer. The British factory in Slough used different colours to suit local tastes; no full list is available.

Year	Model	Body	Wings	Wheels
1934–1936	7	Beige Black	Black	Black (two-tone on Concours d'Elegance models)
		Bordeaux Red Marine Blue Pearl Grey		Black
	7 Cabriolet	Beige Black Bordeaux Red Cream Dark blue Marine Blue Pearl Grey	Black	Black
	7S & 11	Beige Bordeaux Red Marine Blue Olive Green Pearl Grey Sky Blue	Marine Blue	
1937	7	Black Bordeaux Red Marine Blue	Matching body, or Black	Black
	11	Black Bordeaux Red Iridescent Beige Iridescent Grey Marine Blue	Matching body	Matching body
1938–1941	7	Black Iridescent Beige Iridescent Grey Sea Green	Black	Black
	11 Légère	Black Iridescent Beige Iridescent Grey Marine Blue Sea Green	Black	Yellow
	11 Normale	Black Iridescent Grey	Black	Red
	11 Familiale	Black Iridescent Beige Iridescent Green	Matching body	Matching body

Classic Citroëns

	Roadsters (all)	Black Bordeaux Red Iridescent Green Iridescent Grey Marine Blue Olive Green	Matching body, or black	Matching body, but red with black body
	15-Six	Black Bordeaux Red Dark Blue-Green Iridescent Beige Iridescent Dark Grey	Matching body	Ivory
1945–1947	11 (all)	Black Iridescent Dark Grey Iridescent Light Grey Reseda Green	Matching body	Pearl Grey
	15-Six	Black Iridescent Grey	Matching body	Ivory
1948–1952	11 (all)	Black	Matching body	Ivory
	15-Six	Black Metallic Grey	Matching body	Ivory
1953–1954	All	Black Pearl Grey RAF Blue	Matching body	Ivory
1954–1957	11 (all)	Black Heather Grey Iceland Blue Night Blue Pearl Grey	Matching body	Ivory Pearl Grey Iceland Blue Pearl Grey Pearl Grey
	15-Six	Black Heather Grey Iceland Blue Night Blue Pearl Grey Smoky Grey	Matching body	Ivory Pearl Grey Iceland Blue Pearl Grey Pearl Grey Smoky Grey

Paint names in French

English	*French*	*Citroën colour code*
Beige	Beige café-au-lait	
Black	Noir	AC 201
Bordeaux Red	Rouge bordeaux/Rouge excelsior	
Cream	Blanc cassé	
Dark Blue-Green	Blue-vert sombre	
Dark Red	Rouge sang-de-boeuf	
Heather Grey	Gris bruyère	AC 131
Iceland Blue	Bleu d'Islande	AC 122
Iridescent Beige	Beige irisé	
Iridescent Dark Grey	Gris irisé foncé	AC 106
Iridescent Green	Vert irisé	
Iridescent Grey	Gris irisé	AC 109
Iridescent Light Grey	Gris irisé clair	AC 105
Ivory	Ivoire	AC 113
Marine Blue	Bleu marine	
Metallic Grey	Gris métallique	

Night Blue	Bleu nuit	AC 601
Olive Green	Vert olive	
Pearl Grey	Gris Clair/Gris Perle	AC 126
RAF Blue	Bleu RAF	AC 130
Reseda Green	Vert irisé réséda	AC 500
Sea Green	Vert de mer	
Sky Blue	Bleu ciel	
Smoky Grey	Gris fumé	AC 124

THE AUTOCAR, SEPTEMBER 26, 1952

DISTINCTION

with a Difference

The individual and handsome styling of CITROEN gives a distinction that marks it apart from all other cars. But in addition to its external beauty, CITROEN design . . . still the most modern and most successful over the last eighteen years . . . sets it in a different class. Only the fortunate possessors of CITROEN cars are able to appreciate the surging power—the superb, safe road-holding—the effortless high cruising speed —and the wonderful ability that belongs to CITROEN alone to make a smooth run on any road.

FRONT WHEEL DRIVE • INDEPENDENT FRONT SUSPENSION • TORSION BAR SPRINGING
DETACHABLE CYLINDER BARRELS

CITROEN

PRICES
"LIGHT FIFTEEN" SALOON
from £1,067 . 1 . 2
"SIX CYLINDER" SALOON
from £1,525 . 18 . 11
(inc. Purchase Tax)

CITROEN CARS LTD   **SLOUGH   BUCKS**
Telephone : Slough 23811   *Telegrams : Citroworks, Slough*